Family
Warwickshire

Geoff Allen

FAMILY WALKS

HIGH INTEREST · LOW MILEAGE

Scarthin Books of Cromford
Derbyshire
1993

Family Walks in Warwickshire

General Editor: Norman Taylor

The Country Code

Respect the life and work of the countryside
Guard against all risk of fire
Fasten all gates
Keep dogs under close control
Keep to the public paths across farmland
Use gates or stiles to cross fences, hedges and walls
Leave livestock, crops and machinery alone
Take all your litter home
Help to keep all water clean
Protect wildlife, wild plants and trees
Take care on country roads
Make no unnecessary noise

Walking the routes in this book

All the routes in this book have been walked, in most cases, several times prior to publication and we have taken great care to ensure that they are on rights of way. However, changes occur all the time in the landscape; should you meet any obstructions, please let us know. Serious obstructions can be brought to the attention of the local branch of the Ramblers' Association and the Rights of Way section of the County Council.

Published 1993 by Scarthin Books of Cromford, Derbyshire

Printed in Great Britain at The Alden Press, Oxford

ISBN 0907758 533

Cover illustration by Andrew Ravenwood: The Centenary Way, looking towards Ansley Common (Route 4)

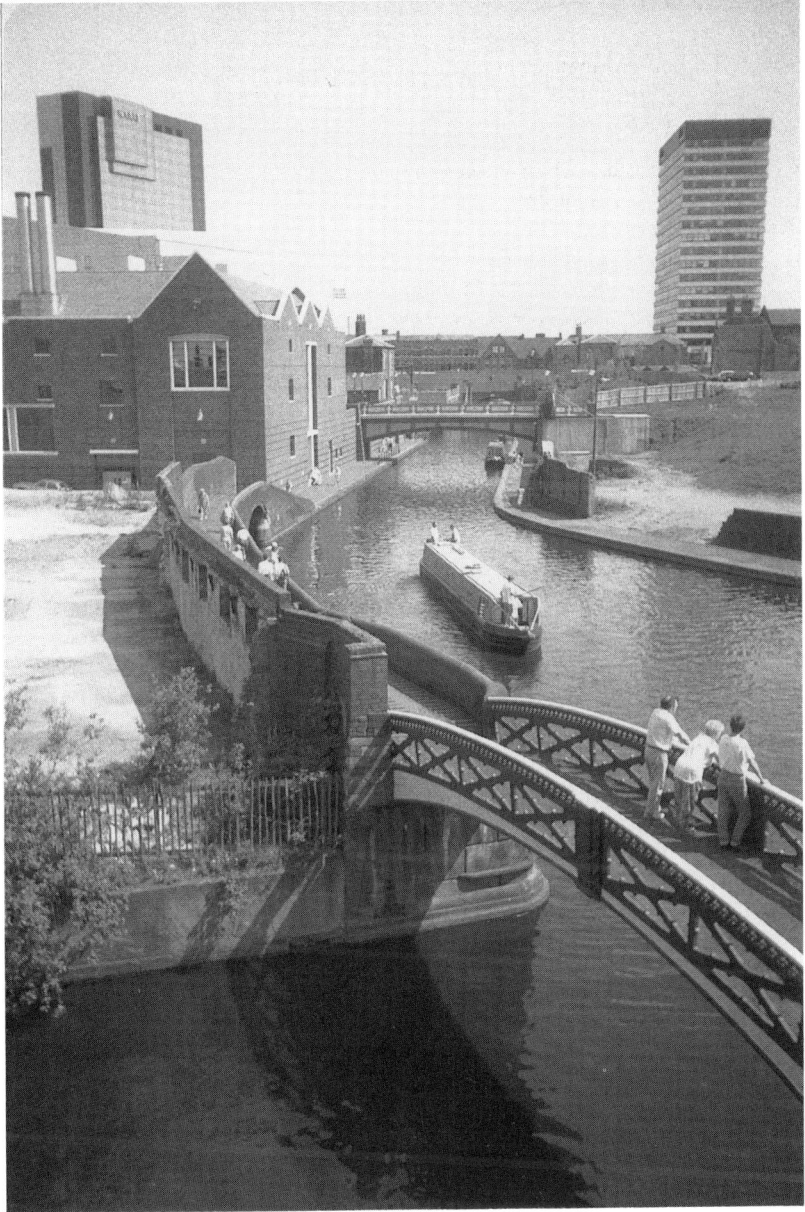

Deep Cutting Junction, looking towards Gas Street Basin (Route 5)

About the author

Geoff Allen is an unfrocked (early-retired) insurance official turned journalist, with over thirty-five years of regular walking behind him. His rambles have been appearing weekly in the *Birmingham Evening Mail* since 1980, and he has long been the Midlands reporter of *The Great Outdoors* magazine.

His previous books were *Out Walking* (1984) and *Midland Hill Walks* (1986), both published by The Birmingham Post & Mail Ltd., and he was a substantial contributor to the AA/OS *Village Walks in Britain* (1991). He also edits *Walker*, the newsletter of the Warwickshire area of the Ramblers' Association.

He enjoys walking in all kinds of countryside, from lowlands to high hills, whether alone or with his wife, Barbara, with his great-nephews Daniel and Nicholas, or with his local rambling club, of which he is secretary.

The former Norman doorway of Alvecote Priory, Shuttington Church (Route 1)

Contents

Map of the area

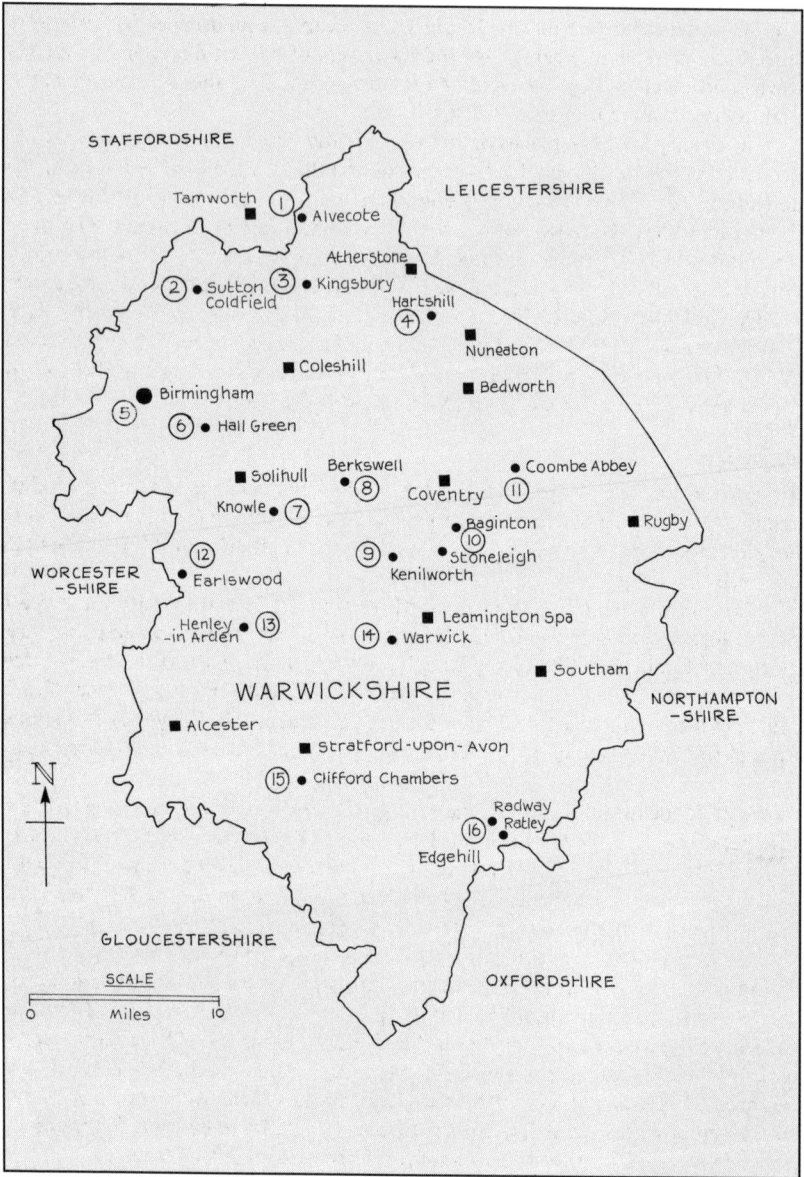

STAFFORDSHIRE

LEICESTERSHIRE

Tamworth ①
● Alvecote

Atherstone

② ● Sutton Coldfield ③ ● Kingsbury

Hartshill
④ ●

Nuneaton

● Coleshill

Bedworth

● Birmingham
⑤ ⑥ ● Hall Green

Berkswell
● Solihull ⑧ ● Coventry ● Coombe Abbey
Knowle ● ⑦ ⑪

Baginton
⑫ ⑨ ● ● Stoneleigh ■ Rugby
WORCESTER -SHIRE ● Earlswood Kenilworth

Henley -in Arden ● ⑬ ● Leamington Spa
⑭ ● Warwick

■ Southam

WARWICKSHIRE

NORTHAMPTON -SHIRE

■ Alcester

■ Stratford-upon-Avon
⑮ ● Clifford Chambers

Radway
⑯ ● Ratley
Edgehill

N

GLOUCESTERSHIRE

OXFORDSHIRE

SCALE
0 Miles 10

Introduction

The County

Though not blessed with any of Britain's more dramatic landscapes, Warwickshire is well-suited for family rambling, and its variety of beautiful scenery, its ancient towns and lovely villages, are certainly better enjoyed by the slow-paced walker than by the rushing motorist.

The county is rich in places of interest of many kinds, and each of the rambles described in this book includes sites (and sights) that should beguile both children and adults. We walk by lakes and alongside rivers and canals; we stroll through old towns and villages with historical associations and the architecture to match them; we follow fieldpaths, tracks and quiet lanes; and we ascend gentle hills to view broad panoramas of the countryside that we have passed through or have still to explore.

This guide covers the old county of Warwickshire as it was before the local government changes of 1974. Thus it includes areas that were then transferred to the West Midlands County Council and, following the demise of that authority, are now administered by Birmingham, Solihull or Coventry.

The Walks

My sixteen rambles are spread around the county and have been selected with the needs of children in mind. They are, however, equally suitable for adults, whether or not accompanied by a child and enjoying the freshness of outlook that a child's presence can bring.

The routes are numbered from north to south. Most are rural, but two are within Birmingham, and you may be surprised to find how interesting they are. Since most families are likely to approach them by car, the walks are all circular, but they are also accessible by public transport (brief details are given at the end of each route description and useful telephone numbers on page 75). They vary in distance from 1½ to 9 miles, though in several cases I have indicated a mileage-saving short-cut.

None of the rambles goes through rough or dangerous country and, except for distances, the differences in standard between them are not great. Nevertheless, under Routes in Order of Difficulty on page 75 I have divided them into four grades to help you decide which to choose. It is advisable, of course, for parties with inexperienced members to start with one of the easier walks.

In some cases a pub lunch can be obtained during the walk, though it is usually advisable to carry a picnic. Stout shoes, fabric boots or even trainers are adequate footwear in dry summer weather, but wet grass, mud or the possibility of rain will call for wellingtons or rambling boots during most of the year. (Please remember to remove muddy footwear when entering pubs, churches and other buildings.) Waterproof clothing should also be carried, unless the forecast guarantees a dry day, together with a small first-aid kit. In case you are lured out only to find that it pours down, a wide range of wet weather alternatives is listed (see page 76).

My route descriptions and sketch maps should be adequate for following the walks, but the relevant 1 : 50,000 scale Ordnance Survey Landranger map (indicated at the start of each route description) should be carried as an additional aid to navigation and to increase interest in the landscape.

The countryside, however, is constantly changing, and it is possible that some features, such as stiles and gates, and the clarity and line of paths, may have altered since I followed the walk. Through the publishers I shall be glad to hear of any changes you may discover.

Since most of the routes include at least one place to linger at, allow plenty of time to complete the walk. Even with older children your pace through fields and over stiles is unlikely to exceed two miles an hour. Add to that the time to be spent on lunch and rest breaks, and at points of interest, and you have a full day out.

Finally, I hope that all these do's and don'ts have not obscured my most important point; that walking in Warwickshire's beautiful countryside is a pleasure well worth the sixteen days it will take you to complete the rambles described here.

Half-timbering – old and new, at Kenilworth

Map symbols

 Route

 Road
Dual-carriageway or motorway

 Track or drive

 Railway

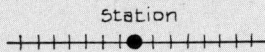 Dismantled railway

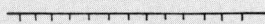 River

 Canal

 Stream

Footbridge

Road bridge

 Lake or pool

Broadleaved woodland

Coniferous woodland

Church with tower

Church with spire

Church without tower or spire

Building

9

Alvecote Priory

Alvecote Pools and railway from the former mine spoil heap

Alvecote Priory and Pools

Outline
Alvecote Priory Picnic Area – Coventry Canal – Amington – Shuttington –
Alvecote Priory Picnic Area.

Summary
An easy ramble, straying into Staffordshire, with some road walking, but mainly
along a canal towpath and level fieldpaths. The climb to Shuttington village can be
avoided by a short cut, saving about ¾ mile. From the picnic area, we follow the
Coventry Canal west to Amington, before looping round through the fields north of
the pools to reach Shuttington by climbing meadows reclaimed from opencast coal
mining. The walk returns to the picnic area by road, via the former mining village of
Alvecote. A second circular ramble of about one mile can be taken round the
neighbouring Warwickshire Wildlife Trust's reserve.

Attractions
The picnic area established by Warwickshire County Council at Alvecote Priory,
near the Staffordshire border, is an excellent place for starting a ramble – or for
delaying the start of one on a fine summer's day, when sitting or playing on the grass
may have a strong appeal.

The small Benedictine priory was established by William Burdet in 1159 as a
Cell to Great Malvern Priory, and was dissolved by Henry VIII in 1536. Not much
remains, most of the buildings having been pulled down about the year 1700, but
there is a good moulded doorway from the late 14th century and a stone dovecote
by the canal. The monks kept pigeons there for fresh winter meat, as well as for eggs
and fertilizer. Before root crops for animal feeding were developed in the 18th
century there were thousands of dovecotes in England.

Across the canal is the Alvecote Pools Nature Reserve, a Site of Special
Scientific Interest. Owned by British Coal and leased to Warwickshire Wildlife
Trust, it can be visited as an extension to the walk (see Route paragraph 7).

The large pools at Alvecote were formed by mining subsidence during World
War II. They are noted for their variety of bird and plant life. One of Britain's first
nature trails was set up here in 1963, and there are guided walks during certain
summer weekends (tel. 0926-496848).

The Coventry Canal was an early waterway, partly opened in 1769. The section
walked had to wait until 1790 for its first traffic, after which it became one of
Britain's most profitable canals. Walking its towpath westwards, we pass a marina.
Beyond, note the contrast between the wild strip of land between the canal and the
railway on one side and the trim golf course across the water. We also pass the
buttresses of a former railway bridge that crossed the canal to a mine.

Shuttington village stands high above the Anker valley. Its little old stone

Continued on page 14

11

Route 1

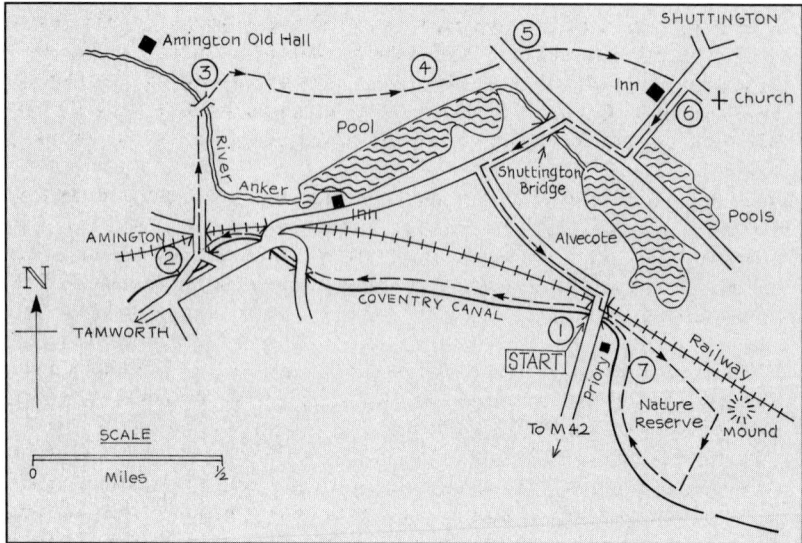

Alvecote Priory and Pools   4 miles or 5 miles

Start

Alvecote Priory Picnic Area, 3 miles east of Tamworth, where a lane crosses the Coventry Canal and the railway (OS Sheets 139 and 140 GR 250043).

Route

1. Go out to the road and cross the canal bridge. Descending to the right, turn under the bridge to follow the towpath west for $1\frac{1}{4}$ miles.

2. At Bridge No. 65 leave the canal and bear right to a little green, backed by cottages. Go right and follow Moor Lane over a railway bridge. Ignore a left turn and keep ahead along an unmade road ending at a stile. Beyond, veer right towards the River Anker and cross it via the footbridge. Downstream the gabled Amington Old Hall can be seen.

3. Follow the right-hand field-edge to a bend on a concrete drive. Climb a stile and turn right to walk along a green track left of a hedge. Stay on the headland path, which swings right and left to reach a stile/gate and continues beside a wire fence. Away to the right is one of the great pools caused by mining subsidence.

12

Route 1 (continued)

4. *Where the fence bears left, keep ahead to a small oak. Passing a pile of rubble on your right (all that remains of Warren Farm), skirt left of woodland and climb a stile. Bear right and walk beside the pool to a lane, where a car-park occupies the site of the former Laundry Cottages. (**A short cut can be made here** by turning right along the lane and right again on rejoining the longer walk at the next junction.)*

5. *Cross the lane to a gate/stile. Bear sharp right over the field to a gate and climb to a gate on the right. Cross a large field to a stile near the right-hand end of buildings at Shuttington, and step over another stile to gain the road by the Wolferstan Arms. (Opposite, a track leads to the churchyard, with its magnificent view of the Alvecote Pools.)*

6. *Take the roadside footpath downhill past the inn, turn right at the T-junction, and left over Shuttington Bridge. Bear left through Alvecote and go over the railway and canal to return to the picnic site.*

7. *For a second circuit of about a mile, starting from the canal bridge, take the public footpath through the Warwickshire Wildlife Trust's nature reserve. On emerging from the trees, it is worth making a diversion along a left-hand path to climb the spoil heap for its all-round views. To continue, however, turn right here. At a cross-track go right for a few yards, then off left and down to cross a footbridge. Follow the path through trees and, soon climbing to the canal bank, walk it to the right, back to the road bridge.*

Access by bus
Mercian service: Tamworth – Amington – Shuttington.

13

church contains a Norman doorway brought from Alvecote Priory, and the churchyard provides a magnificent view of the pools. Along the nature reserve circuit notice the stunted oaks and, on the spoil heap, look for black wolf spiders – became an arachnidophile!

Refreshments

The Wolferstan Arms, Shuttington (bar meals). Village stores at Shuttington and Alvecote.

Lord Donegal's Ride and the Ebrook (route 2)

Sutton Park

Outline
Town Gate – Holly Hurst – Jamboree Memorial – Rowton's Hill – Icknield Street – Streetly Gate – Bracebridge Pool – Blackroot Pool – Town Gate.

Summary
A walk through the heathland, woods and wetlands making up the 2,400 acres of one of Britain's largest urban parks, designated as a Site of Special Scientific Interest. The hills are small and gentle, we visit three of the Park's half-dozen large pools, and there are opportunities for refreshments and toilet stops. Though all facilities may not be open in winter, the Park's ease of access to the vast Birmingham and Black Country population makes it especially suitable for walking during the shorter days, and its abundance of holly (but not for picking, please!) adds to the seasonal flavour of a Christmas stroll.

Attractions
Nearly 500 years after Bishop Vesey of Exeter – a local Sutton lad who had made good – persuaded Henry VIII to grant a royal charter to Sutton Coldfield, Sutton Park remains a green oasis within the built-up West Midlands. It is large enough to attract the serious rambler, as well as the stroller content with a circuit of around a mile or so.

The Park was once a royal forest, or hunting ground for the king. In 1126 it came into the ownership of the Earl of Warwick and, being no longer royal, was downgraded from "forest" to "chase". Under Henry VIII's royal charter of 1528, the chase was given to the townspeople of Sutton Coldfield for ever. In the 18th century the Park survived a proposal by Sir Joseph Scott of Great Barr Hall that it should be enclosed and divided up between local landowners, but Victorian conservationists were less successful in 1879 when, amid great controversy, the Midland Railway Company's Birmingham to Walsall line was driven through its north-eastern fringe. Fortunately the scars on the landscape have long since healed and the railway now seems part of the scenery.

In 1957 the World Jubilee Jamboree of the Scout Movement was held in the Park. We pass its commemorative plaque on our walk.

Other features of interest include the Roman road, Icknield Street, which follows the western edge of the Park as part of its journey from Gloucestershire to Yorkshire, and Rowton's Well. We can imagine Roman legionaries camping on nearby Rowton's Hill and using the well, which can be seen within wooden fencing about 300 yards to the south. Between the hill and Icknield Street we follow Lord Donegal's Ride. His lordship lived at Fisherwick Hall, near Lichfield, in the 18th century and used the Ride when hunting in the Park. The Ride passes the Butts, an

Continued on page 18

15

Route 2

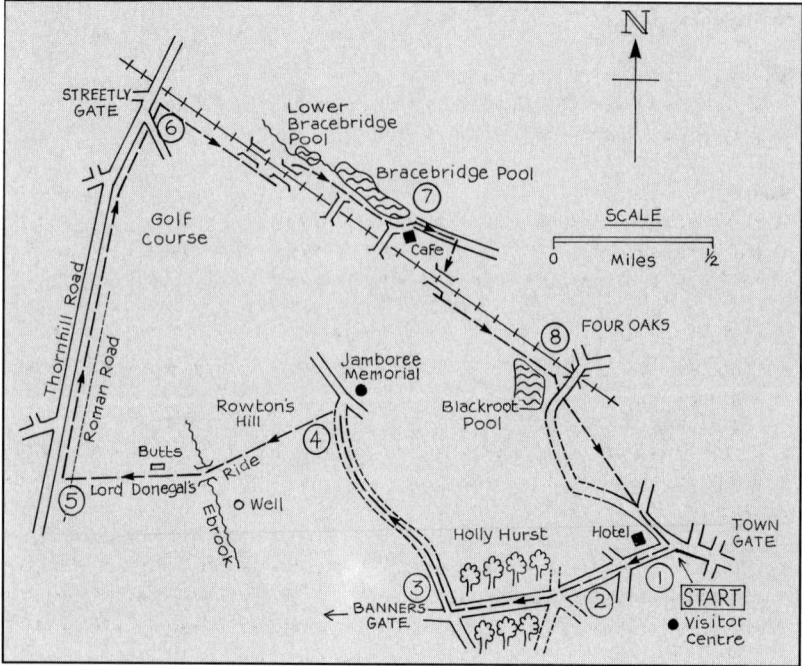

Route 2

Sutton Park

$6\frac{1}{2}$ miles

Start

Town Gate, Tudor Hill, Sutton Coldfield (OS Sheet 139 GR 116964; 6" to 1 mile Map of Sutton Park).

Route

1. *Enter Town Gate and, if travelling by car, park within (free). Continue on foot along the road and fork left for 300 yards to a wooden gate barring vehicles. Away to the left is the circular Visitor Centre.*

2. *Follow the "Pedestrians Banners Gate" pointer ahead and take the surfaced way to the wooded Holly Hurst. At the 5-way junction go straight ahead to climb the broad Wyndley Glade.*

3. *Emerging from the trees at a cross-roads, turn right along a surfaced way, passing a vehicle barrier and continuing between woods and heathland. Just beyond another vehicle barrier is the Scout Jamboree Memorial.*

4. *Turn left along a broad, straight track through silver birches to Rowton's Hill, with the distant, pine-capped Barr Beacon visible slightly to the right. Descend the track ahead (Lord Donegal's Ride), cross a bridge over the Ebrook and pass the Butts on your right.*

5. *About 100 yards before Royal Oak Gate, cross the slightly raised Icknield Street (Roman road). Continue and turn right along the perimeter path, skirting the golf course opened in 1893, to reach Streetly Gate (toilets).*

6. *Cross the road and bear right beside railway lines. Go left through the second railway arch to Lower Bracebridge Pool. Turn right and take a broad track, with the main Bracebridge Pool glimpsed through trees. Turn left beside the end of the pool to a cafe, refreshment kiosk and toilets, noting the information board along the way.*

7. *Beyond the cafe follow the road to a parking area. Descend a rough track to your right, pass under a railway arch and turn left to reach Blackroot Pool.*

8. *Keeping left of the pool, cross a road and veer to the right over high grassland (the site of a Victorian race-course). Descend to Holly Knoll car park and bear left along the road back to Town Gate, passing the entrance to Park House Hotel.*

old concrete trench amid pine trees on its north side, used for rifle training by the Army in Victorian times and during World War I. There is a great deal of history to stimulate the mind whilst we walk in the lovely and peaceful acres of Sutton Park.

Refreshments
Park House, near Town Gate; Bobby Brown's Cafe and kiosk, by Bracebridge Pool.

Guidebook
Sutton Park: Its History and Wildlife by Douglas V. Jones. Westwood Press Publications.

Access by train and bus
Trains (Birmingham New Street–Lichfield line) to Sutton Coldfield Station, $\frac{1}{4}$-mile from Town Gate.

Buses, WMT services run from the City Centre and many other points to Sutton Coldfield, for Town Gate, and to other gates of the Park.

Kingsbury Church and Manor across Hemlingford Water

18

Kingsbury Water Park

Outline
Visitor Centre – Bodymoor Heath Water – Kingsbury Church –
River Tame – Far Leys Car-park – Pools – Birmingham & Fazeley Canal –
Broomycroft Car-park – Pools – Woodland Walk – Visitor Centre.

Summary
Level walking on good paths between pools and by the River Tame, and along the
Birmingham & Fazeley Canal towpath, but there is a long flight of steps to climb for
the optional diversion to Kingsbury Church. Included in the ramble is the Water
Park's $1\frac{1}{2}$ mile Winter Walk circuit, which is fully described in a booklet on sale at
the shop near the main entrance. The Park's *Find Your Way Around* leaflet, which
includes an 8″ to 1 mile map, is useful for this walk.

Bus travellers
Alight in Kingsbury village and join the walk at the church.

Attractions
There are more than 30 lakes and pools in the 600-acre Kingsbury Water Park,
which Warwickshire County Council has been developing since 1973 in the Tame
valley, between Birmingham and Tamworth. The result of half-a-century of gravel
extraction, now landscaped and set among grass and trees, they attract both
humans and wildlife.

For a family day out, the Water Park offers miles of waterside and woodland
walks, plus games and picnic areas, an adventure playground, boating pools, a
visitor centre and cafe (not open in winter), exhibitions and a shop. Make a day of it
and combine the short walk described overleaf with enjoyment of the Park's other
facilities. The shop sells useful leaflets, including a description of a nature trail
opened by TV naturalist Phil Drabble in 1990, and there are guide booklets
describing walks for each of the four seasons.

On the walk there is free childrens' fishing and an adventure playground at Far
Leys, plus boating on nearby Mitchells Pool. Overlooking the large, irregularly
shaped Cliff Pool are wooden hides from which visitors can watch the many birds
on the water without disturbing them. The embankment round the pool was
constructed to screen the wildfowl from human interference. The Park also has a
model boating pool, reached by following the drive to the right from the main
entrance.

The Birmingham & Fazeley Canal was designed by the engineer John Smeaton
and completed in 1789. It is a link canal, connecting Birmingham City Centre (see
Route 5) with the Coventry Canal at Fazeley, near Tamworth, and with the Trent &
Mersey at Fradley Junction. Curdworth Bottom Lock, which we pass, is the first of

Continued on page 22

Route 3

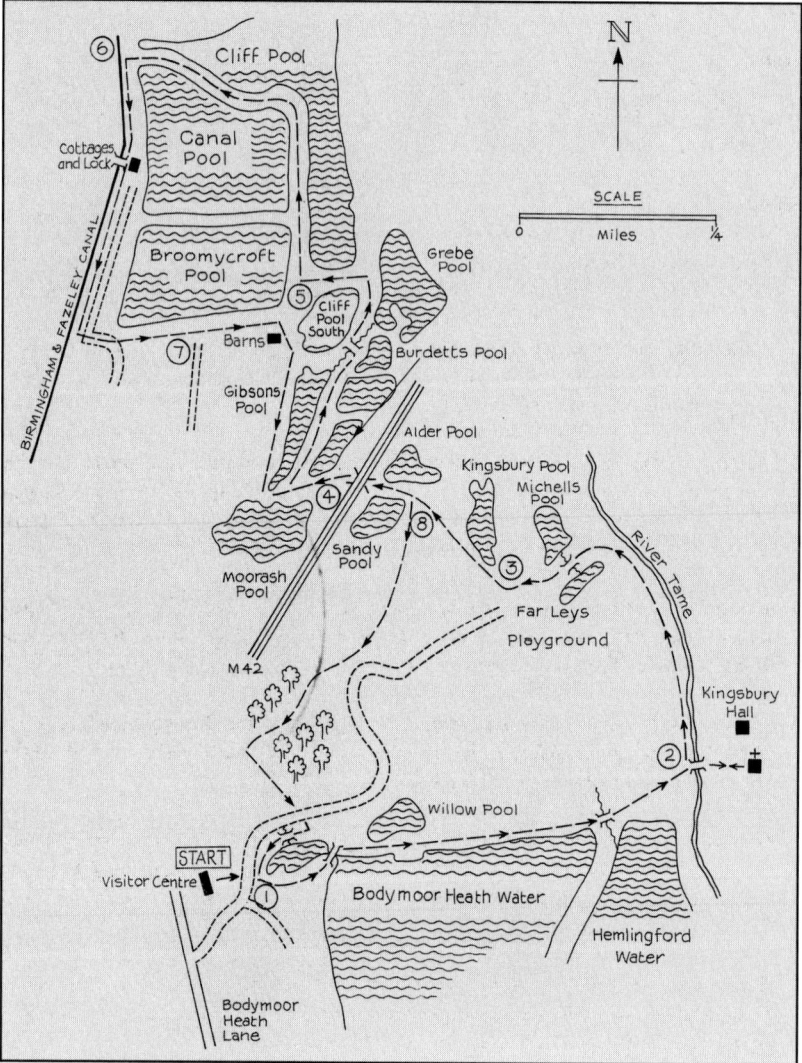

Route 3

Kingsbury Water Park

4 or $1\frac{3}{4}$ miles

Start

Visitor Centre pay car-park, off Bodymoor Heath Lane, between A4091 and A4097 (OS Sheet 139 GR 204959), or free car-park, Pear Tree Avenue, Kingsbury village (GR 218965).

Route

1. *Cross the drive and pick up a gravel path skirting left of Bodymoor Heath Water. Cross a footbridge and follow a causeway to a bridge over the River Tame. Beyond, steps rise to Kingsbury churchyard, and the Elizabethan manor to the north.*

2. *Return and recross the river, bearing right along its bank. Go left between two pools to a railed footbridge and continue across grassland to a track leading to Far Leys car-park and adventure playground.*

3. *Just before the car-park turn right along a broad path. Pass Kingsbury Pool. (* **For a short cut** *reducing the walk to $1\frac{3}{4}$ miles, turn sharp left, following the Woodland Walk – see paragraph 8). Go between Alder and Sandy pools (all names are signposted) to a tunnel under the M42.*

4. *Emerging, keep ahead, then turn right between Burdetts and Gibsons pools. In just under $\frac{1}{4}$ mile cross a railed bridge on the left to Cliff Pool South. Here join the Winter Walk, following it anti-clockwise round the pool to Waymark 4.*

5. *The trail bears right, between the embanked Cliff Pool and Broomycroft Pool, then skirts Canal Pool. Turn left at the end, passing bird-watchers' hides, and follow the shore to the Birmingham & Fazeley Canal.*

6. *Go left along the towpath, past the cottages at Curdworth Bottom Lock, and at Waymark 6 join the access road. Follow it to a right-hand bend, go straight ahead over a stile and continue along a path between a young plantation and a hedge to Broomycroft car-park.*

7. *Keep ahead past Waymark 1 to Waymark 2 at Cliff Pool South and bear right, passing 18th century barns. At Waymark 7 turn right, between Gibsons Pool and a meadow, then left to return through the M42 tunnel.*

8. *Beyond Sandy Pool take a path on the right, following the Woodland Walk and emerging from the trees to pass near a bend in a drive. Keep to the path, which meanders through more woodland and meets the drive further south. Cross to a path running parallel to the drive and go over a bridge to the right. The path now curves to the left and leads back to the Visitor Centre.*

21

13, heading south, that raise the level 76 feet in $2\frac{1}{2}$ miles. The lock-keeper's cottage is dated MDCCCXX (1820) in Roman numerals – our modern high-tech age could not have developed if the Arabs hadn't devised our present system of numbers!

The eastern side of the Water Park is bordered by the broad River Tame, which flows north through Tamworth to feed the Trent. Silhouetted on a bank high above it is Kingsbury's great church of Norman origin. Its doorway is of that period, but the tower is 14th century and the belfry was built 200 years later. Beside the churchyard is the long stone wall of the Elizabethan hall, now a farmhouse, where the Saxon kings of Mercia are said to have built a palace.

Refreshments
Cafe at Visitor Centre in summer; inns (bar meals) at Kingsbury village.

Access by bus
Mercian service: Birmingham – Kingsbury village – Tamworth.

Kingsbury Manor

22

Hartshill Hayes and the Centenary Way

Outline

Hartshill Hayes Country Park – Ansley Common – Church End – Hoar
Park Wood – Birchley Heath – Hartshill Hayes.

Summary

A rather hilly walk, mostly waymarked. It is somewhat longer than other walks, but
includes fine elevated stretches and can be greatly shortened, as indicated in the
route description. From Hartshill Hayes Country Park, between Nuneaton and
Atherstone, a section of the Centenary Way long-distance footpath leads to the
former mining village of Ansley Common. We climb fields and join the B4114 to
Church End, continuing to Hoar Park Wood, from which we return along the
Centenary Way to our starting point.

Attractions

From the county council's Hartshill Hayes Country Park there are immense views
north, across the Anker valley, to the rocky tors of Charnwood Forest in
Leicestershire. It is said that forty churches can be seen from the hilltop. How many
can you count?

The 550ft-high ridge attracted dwellers in the Stone and Bronze ages, when it
stood clear and dry above the lowland forests and marshes. There are signs of a hillfort constructed by the Celts in the centuries before Christ, and in 1125 Hugh de
Hardreshull built a castle there.

The 100-mile Centenary Way footpath commemorates the hundredth anniversary of the county council in 1989. Starting from Kingsbury Water Park (see Route
3) the waymarked path winds south to the edge of the Cotswolds at Meon Hill.
Guide leaflets to it can be purchased at the Country Park.

Look out for unusual animals at Moorwood Rare Breed Leisure Farm. The
ancient church at Church End was once owned by Lady Godiva, and our fieldpath
from it leads to Ansley Mill, which occupies a mill site used since the 12th century.
Hoar Park Wood is a surviving fragment of the ancient Forest of Arden and a Site
of Special Scientific Interest.

Refreshments

Hartshill Hayes Country Park (when ranger present).

23

Route 4

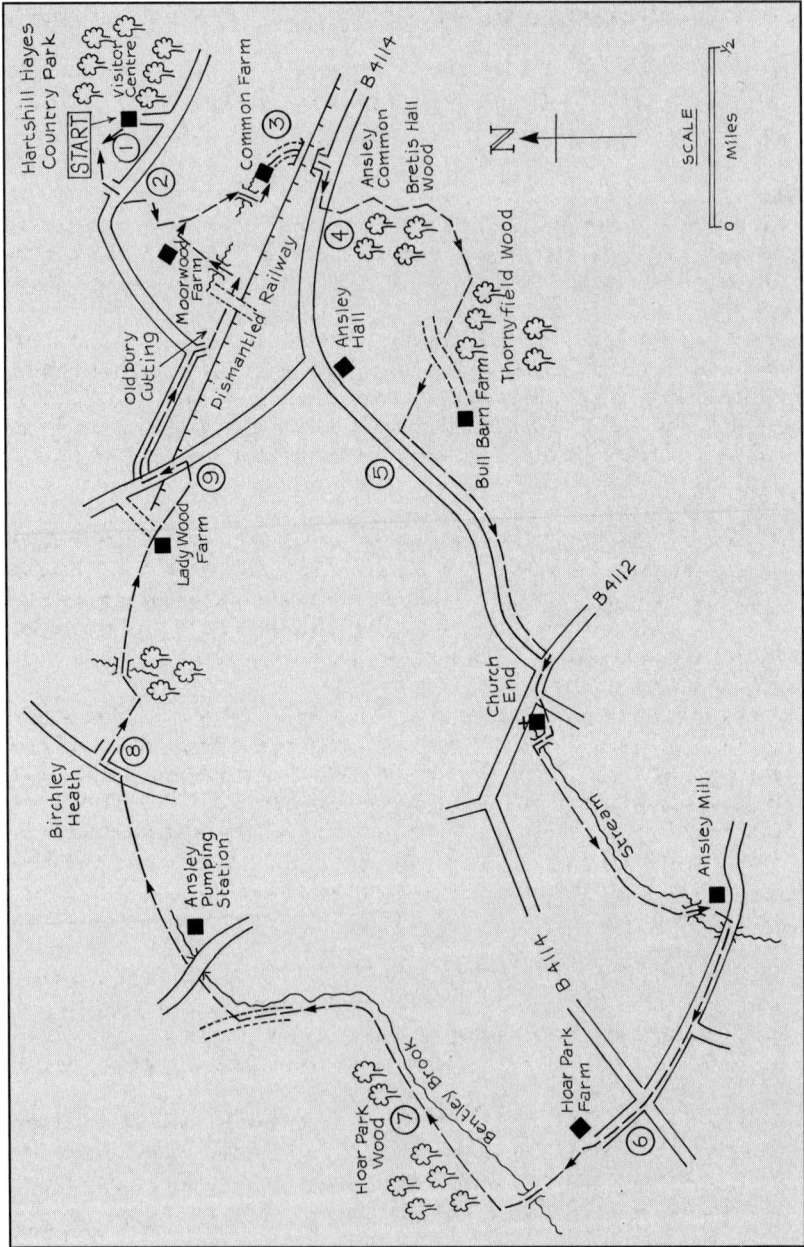

Route 4

Hartshill Hayes and the Centenary Way $3\frac{1}{4}$ miles or 9 miles

Start

Pay car-park at Hartshill Hayes Country Park, $3\frac{1}{2}$ miles north-west of Nuneaton (OS Sheet 140 GR 315946).

Route

1. *From the Visitor Centre follow the St Lawrence Walk's direction post No. 1, at the far side of the car-park. Skirt a covered reservoir on your left and turn left through a gate to a lane.*

2. *From a stile opposite, cross the field diagonally and go over a rise to a stile. Descend an enclosed path towards Moorwood Farm, then turn left along a fenced track, passing a narrow pool. Bearing right to a stile, gate and second stile, cross the end of a field to a stile and short plank footbridge. In the next field go left along the hedge and turn right at the corner to a stile on the left. Cross it and bear right to a stile at Common Farm.*

3. *Follow the farm drive under the railway bridge to Ansley Common, a former mining village on the B4114, and turn right along the roadside footpath for 200 yards. (**For a short cut** reducing the walk to $3\frac{1}{4}$ miles, continue for another $\frac{1}{2}$ mile alongside the B4114 and turn right into a lane. After a further $\frac{1}{2}$ mile rejoin the longer walk just before the turn to Oldbury Cutting Picnic Area – see paragraph 9.)*

4. *For the longer walk, follow the Centenary Way sign left at Limes Coppice to a stile and climb to the left to reach a stile in the projecting upper hedge. Ascend left of a hedge and, where it ends, veer right to a stile in the facing hedge. Skirt Bret's Hall Wood to a gate/stile on the right and descend a field to a stile. Here leave the Centenary Way by climbing a tractor track to a gate at the top right of the field. Follow the left-hand field-edge past Thornyfield Wood, and cross the Bull Barn Farm track to a stile. Go through the field beyond, aiming for a stile on the B4114, right of woodland.*

5. *Follow the roadside footpath left to Church End. Walk through the churchyard to a stile and cross a railed footbridge. Follow the stream, left, to Ansley Mill, passing woodlands and a pond, and crossing another railed bridge. At the mill cross a plank footbridge and a stile, and bear right to a stile on a lane. Turn right to the B4114.*

6. *Cross the B4114 and descend Hoar Park Farm drive, passing left of the farmhouse to a gate. Turn left down a large field to reach doublegates and a bridge over Bentley Brook, and climb to the corner of Hoar Park Wood, rejoining the Centenary Way and bearing right along it.*

Continued on page 26

25

7. *Immediately before a copse, change sides of the hedge at a stile and follow the right-hand edge of a vast field. Go through a gate to join a track for just over 200 yards, take a signed path from a stile on the right and follow a field-edge to a lane. To the right is Ansley Pumping Station, from beside which an old pack-horse trail will lead you to another former mining village, Birchley Heath.*

8. *There, turn left along the lane, and take the first road on the right. At the end continue beside a hedge to a wood. Bear left to a stile, and cross a field corner to a plank footbridge and stile. Go down a long field to Lady Wood Farm and over its drive to a stile and signed path, leading to a stile on the left. Cross a field to a stile on a lane, where the shorter walk comes in from the right.*

9. *Turn left, then first right to Oldbury Cutting Picnic Area, where the Centenary Way is signed along a former colliery railway embankment. After climbing the third stile, take a stile on the left with a white waymark, indicating a concessionary path. Descend to cross a plank footbridge and stiles. Climb the field right of Moorwood Farm, where the Centenary Way is arrowed, right, along the top hedge to the short plank footbridge and stile mentioned in paragraph 2. From it retrace your steps to the country park.*

Access by train and bus

Train to Nuneaton or Atherstone. Midland Red from Coventry, Nuneaton or Atherstone to Hartshill village (1 mile from country park), or Ansley Common.

Hartshill Hayes Country Park

Birmingham Canal Walk

Outline

Birmingham City Centre – Centenary Square – International Convention Centre – Gas Street Basin – Birmingham & Fazeley Canal – Digbeth Branch Canal – Birmingham City Centre.

Summary

An urban walk of great interest, combining the old and new of England's second city. After passing through Centenary Square and the International Convention Centre, we follow canal towpaths to Aston Junction and Warwick Bar, from which it is a short stroll back into the city centre. The towpaths have been restored for walking, but care is, of course, necessary with young children.

Attractions

We start near the very centre of our national waterways system; for the Birmingham Canal Navigations Society's signpost at Deep Cutting Junction marks what has been called the cross-roads of England's canals. The Gas Street Basin to Aston Junction section of the Birmingham & Fazeley Canal and the connecting Digbeth Canal were declared conservation areas and opened up for walking by Birmingham Inner City Partnership in 1987. Useful illustrated leaflets (*Birmingham Canal Walkway Guides, Nos. 1 and 3,* and *Canals in Birmingham*) are available from information centres, the City Development Department (tel. 021-235-3654) and British Waterways (021-633-3666).

The Birmingham & Fazeley was built by the engineer John Smeaton. Opened in 1789, it links the city with the Coventry Canal at Fazeley, near Tamworth, and was so successful that 24-hour working had to be introduced over the stretch we follow to Aston Junction. The canal passes through varied urban scenery – the old canal basin at Gas Street, the new International Convention Centre and the National Indoor Arena, the 18th century canal buildings at Cambrian Wharf, the concrete canyon of Canning Walk, Victorian factories, and the contrastingly modern Aston Science Park at the junction with the Digbeth Branch Canal.

The Digbeth Branch came into use in 1799 as a short cut between the Warwick & Birmingham Canal (now part of the Grand Union) and the Birmingham & Fazeley. It passes through the Ashted Tunnel, which at 103 yards is just short enough for the railed towpath to be walked without a torch. Effectively, another short tunnel is formed by the adjacent railway bridges built for the Grand Junction Railway (1838) from Liverpool and the London & Birmingham Railway of 1854. Immediately before we leave the canal is the Birmingham Gun Barrel Proof House (1813).

Continued on page 30

27

Route 5

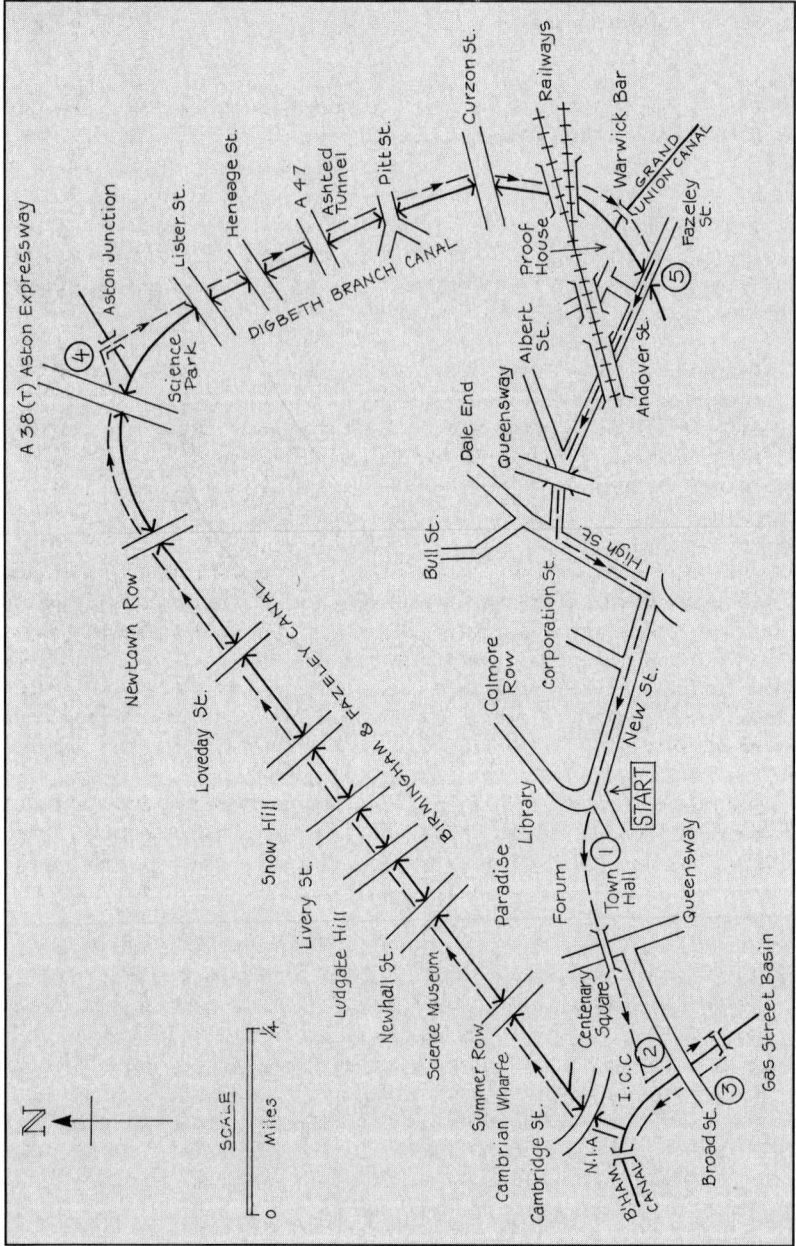

Route 5

Birmingham Canal Walk $4\frac{1}{4}$ miles

Start

Victoria Square, by Town Hall, at junction of Colmore Row and New Street (OS Sheet 139 GR 067868; Birmingham A–Z).

Route

1. *Climb steps towards the Public Library and enter the Paradise Forum doors to the left of it. Walk through to the far exit and, passing the glass-surfaced Copthorne Hotel, cross the bridge over Queensway to Centenary Square.*

2. *Ahead rises the International Convention Centre. Pass through it to the far side, emerging above the canal, and follow the waterway left, under Broad Street Tunnel, to Gas Street Basin. Skirt the basin and cross a bridge on your right to reach the far side of the canal at Worcester Bar. (If the ICC is closed, go left to Broad Street, right along it to the canal bridge and descend steps on the right to the towpath.)*

3. *Double back under the tunnel to Deep Cutting Junction and briefly bear left along the Birmingham Canal to a cast-iron bridge (Horseley Iron Works, 1827). Cross and turn right to join the Birmingham & Fazeley Canal, which is followed to Aston Junction. Diversions may be made to enjoy the views from the terrace surrounding the National Indoor Arena, to cross Tindal Bridge (Cambridge Street) to the old buildings of Cambrian Wharf, and to visit the Museum of Science & Industry in Newhall Street.*

4. *After passing under the A38(T) Aston Expressway, cross another cast-iron bridge to join the Digbeth Branch Canal. Follow it past a junction with the Grand Union Canal (just along which can be seen the Warwick Bar toll island) to the end of the towpath at Fazeley Street, immediately after passing the Birmingham Gun Barrel Proof House of 1813 on your right.*

5. *Turn right up the street, right again into Andover Street and right at the end of it into Banbury Street to view the attractive Dutch-style entrance of the Proof House. Return to Fazeley Street and continue uphill. Join Albert Street and go left under Queensway to Dale End. Turn left to High Street and follow it to New Street, on the right, which leads back to Victoria Square.*

Our walk crosses Birmingham's new Centenary Square. Though it has been praised as an open space, there has been controversy about its 30ft-long glass-fibre group of industrial figures entitled Forward (which is also the city's motto). Across the square is the magnificent International Convention Centre, opened in 1991. Its ground floor is open to the public and we walk through.

Another major new building, the National Indoor Arena, is passed on the Birmingham & Fazeley Canal walk. There are impressive views from its terrace of the canal below and the city skyline. It is also worth breaking the walk to visit the Museum of Science & Industry. The vast collection ranges from bicycles to steam engines (normally in steam on the first and third Wednesdays of each month). It includes a scale model of the Birmingham Canal Navigations system, which offers over a hundred miles of fascinating towpath walking, of which the following is just a sample.

Refreshments

Pubs and cafes in Birmingham city centre; cafes at Birmingham International Convention Centre; light refreshments at the Museum of Science & Industry; James Brindley pub at Gas Street Basin.

'The crossroads of England's canals' – Birmingham Canal Navigation Society signpost at Deep Cutting Junction (Route 5)

Sarehole Mill and the River Cole

Outline
Sarehole Mill – River Cole – Trittiford Mill Park – The Dingles – Sarehole Mill.

Summary
A level walk beside the clear and swift little River Cole and round the lovely Trittiford Mill Pool. It is ideal for families with young children and is possible with pushchairs in dry conditions. The walk can be extended along the river to the south of Scriber's Lane and to the north of Sarehole Mill. The *Birmingham A–Z* will be useful.

Attractions
The ground covered by the walk is a remarkable example of how channels of greenery can survive within industrial cities. At the turn of the century, when J. R. R. Tolkien, author of *The Hobbit* and *The Lord of the Rings*, lived as a child in what is now Wake Green Road, the areas was still rural, and he has described how memories of it influenced him when writing his highly popular books. Hall Green was then in Worcestershire; it did not become part of Warwickshire until 1911. After the opening of the Birmingham to Stratford railway line in 1907, the city suburbs flowed south to engulf most of the fields and woods. Fortunately some green patches remain to give us an idea of the countryside Tolkien knew. The city council is promoting the Cole Valley as a walkway, both here, in its western section between the Ackers Trust and Yardley Wood, and to the east under Project Kingfisher, between Stechford and Bacon's End.

Sarehole Mill is one of the few places in Hall Green that Tolkien would recognise today. A restored 18th century water-mill, it belongs to the city council and is among the handful of survivors from more than seventy mills once operating in the Birmingham area. As is often the case, a mill existed on the site long before the present buildings were constructed. They date from the 1760s and ended their commercial life in 1919. The 1960s saw them restored as a working mill, and today channels of flowing water and numerous massive, revolving wheels can be seen. The water's source is a large pond behind the mill. Old tools, pictures and displays illustrate the history and techniques of milling.

Children can now be taken to Sarehole Mill without experiencing the fright that young Tolkien had on seeing the father and son who then operated it. He later described them as "characters of wonder and terror to a small child", and remembered how the father had a black beard, though the son – a "white ogre" in his clothes covered with flour dust – was far more frightening. The mill is open from 2 to 5 pm, late March to end of October. Admission free.

The late comedian Tony Hancock was born nearby at 41 Southam Road. Go

Continued on page 34

31

Route 6

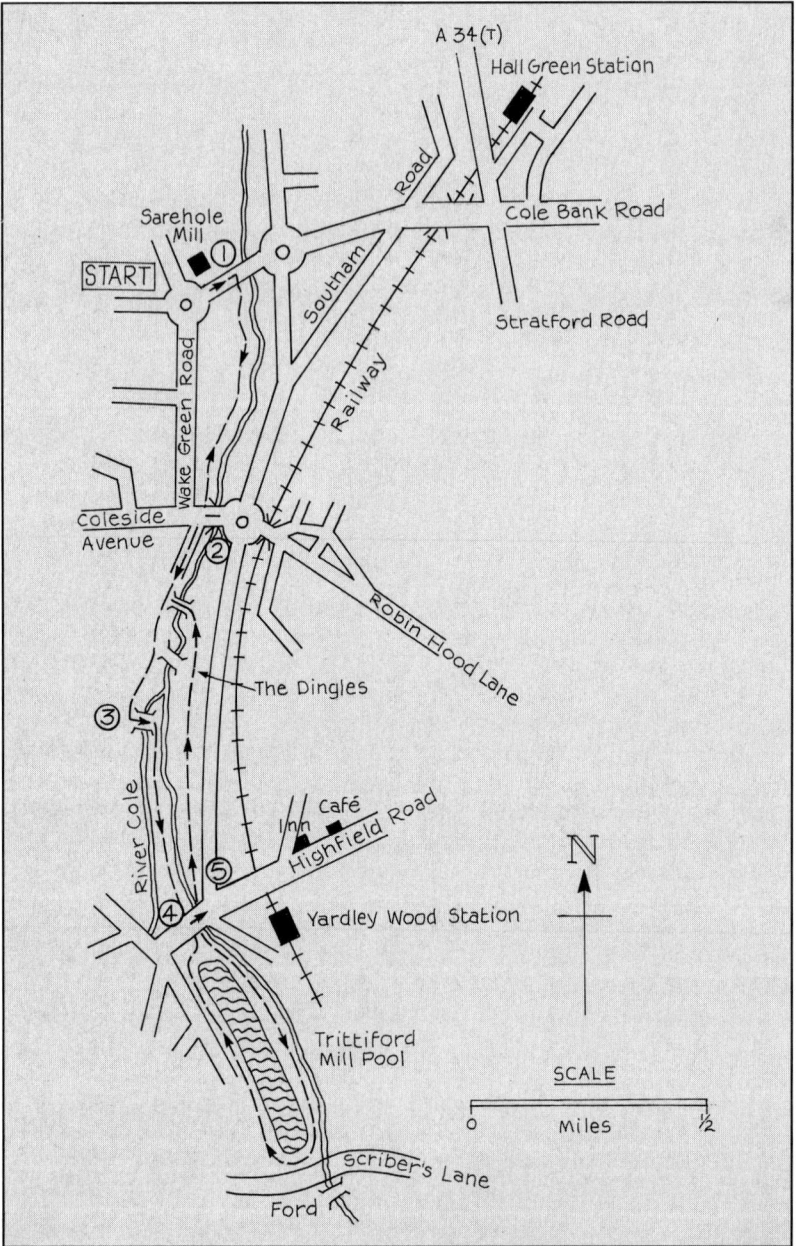

Route 6

Sarehole Mill and the River Cole   3 miles

Start

From free car-park, Sarehole Mill Recreation Ground, Cole Bank Road, Hall Green, Birmingham (OS Sheet 139 GR 099818; Birmingham A–Z).

Route

1. *Go out to the road and turn right for Sarehole Mill. After visiting the mill, cross the road and take the gravel path opposite the car-park, which meanders through the Cole valley beside the river, to Robin Hood Lane. (A few yards to the right, in Wake Green Road, a row of post-World War II "pre-fabs" can still be seen – a rare survival.)*

2. *Cross Robin Hood Lane to Coleside Avenue, a cul-de-sac, and walk along it. At the end, pass Four Arches Bridge on your left (you will cross it from the other side later), and skirt right of trees. Pass a second bridge, follow the path down an avenue between trees and continue through a broad green area to a railed footbridge on the left.*

3. *Cross the bridge and turn right along a path, with water flowing on each side (a mill-race was constructed in the 18th century to increase the supply to Sarehole Mill), leading to Highfield Road. (Families with pushchairs will find the going easier if they ignore the bridge and continue through the grassy area to the road.)*

4. *Cross the road and the grass beyond it to reach the long, narrow Trittiford Mill Pool. Walk clockwise round the water to Scriber's Lane at the far end, and turn left to visit the ford. Return to the pool and complete the circuit of it through Trittiford Mill Park to Highfield Road.*

5. *Cross to the right of the River Cole and walk beside it through the long green strip known as The Dingles. At the far end, return to Coleside Avenue via Four Arches Bridge (a brick structure resembling an old pack-horse bridge) on your left, and follow the outward route back to Sarehole Mill.*

Access by train and bus

Trains (Birmingham Snow Hill–Stratford line) to Hall Green, $\frac{1}{2}$ mile from Sarehole Mill, or Yardley Wood, 300 yards from River Cole in Highfield Road.

Buses WMT services from the city centre and along the Outer Circle to Cole Bank Road.

left from Sarehole Mill along Cole Bank Road, cross Sarehole Road to Southam Road and turn left to No. 41 on the far side (plaque on wall).

Trees and shrubs line the river between Sarehole Mill and Trittiford Mill Pool, and in the long green meadows there is evidence of an old ridge and furrow system.

Though it long ago lost its mill, Trittiford Mill Pool has a lovely, wooded setting and is noted for its bird life. The ford in Scriber's Lane, at its southern end, is an unusual feature for a modern city suburb.

Refreshments
Pub and cafe in Highfield Road, east of River Cole.

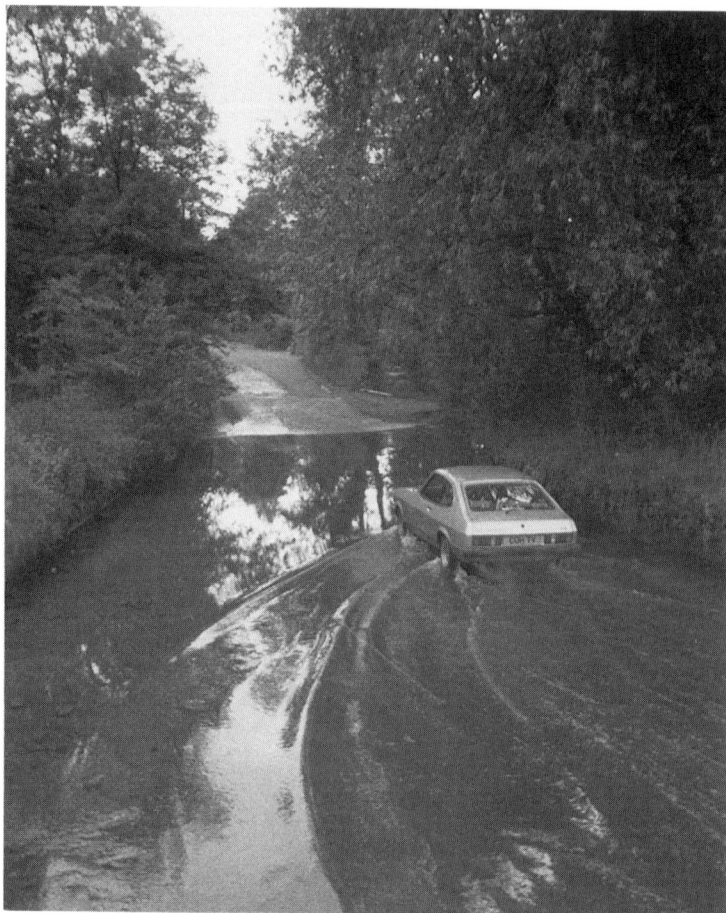

The ford, Scriber's Lane

Knowle and Temple Balsall

Outline

Knowle – Barston – Temple Balsall – Knowle.

Summary

A walk on fieldpaths, a canal towpath and quiet lanes through gently undulating countryside to the east of Knowle. We climb to the churchyard at Barston for its wide-ranging views (there is a useful seat for a coffee or lunch break, and a nearby inn), and visit impressive old almshouses and the church of the Knights Templar at Temple Balsall. Wellies are recommended after prolonged wet weather, because fields near the River Blythe can flood, as can part of the green lane from Piercil End.

Attractions

Gypsies, navvies and medieval knights are our companions on this ramble. We meet the first at Knowle, where the magnificent church, dating from 1402, has the tomb of a gypsy king, Lawrence Boswell, and his son of the same name, outside its south wall. Only rarely can an ancient church be so precisely dated, but we know that it was built by locally-born Walter Cook, who had risen to be a Canon of the Church and a wealthy man. He also paid for the fine Guild House next door.

The navvies (short for navigators) built Britain's network of canals in the late 18th and early 19th centuries. We see some of their work when walking the towpath of the Grand Union Canal. The Grand Union Canal Company was formed in 1929 by combining several canals. The section we follow was originally part of the Warwick & Birmingham Canal, opened in 1800.

Temple Balsall is an exciting place for anybody with a historical imagination, and a lovely one even to those who lack it. For between the quadrangle of almshouses for poor women – the Lady Katherine Leveson Hospital of 1678 – and the Old Hall stands the great church of the Knights Templar (or, perhaps, of their successors the Hospitallers). Also known as the Knights of St John, the Hospitallers were the forerunners of today's St John's Ambulance Brigade. The Templars were a band of soldier priests formed in 1118 to protect pilgrims to the Holy Land, and as such fought in the Crusades. They acquired land at Balsall in 1146 and it became one of their major bases until the order was disbanded in 1308. Their possessions were transferred by order of the Pope to the Hospitallers, who remained at Temple Balsall until about 1470. The church was restored in the late 1840s. Its varying floor levels are unusual, as is the lack of aisles and transepts in so large a building.

The Old Hall is a survival of the Hospitallers' days. Lady Katherine Leveson, who endowed the hospital, was a grand-daughter of Queen Elizabeth's Robert Dudley, Earl of Leicester, who lived at Kenilworth Castle (see Route 9). The path we follow from the almshouses to the Old Hall is known as The Breadwalk, because the women used it when collecting their bread allowance from the bailiff.

Route 7

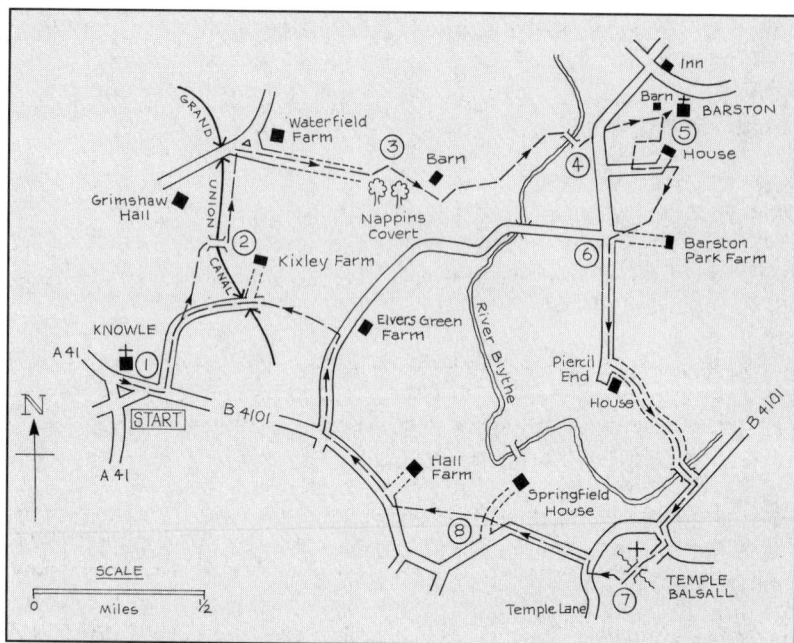

The Breadwalk, with Almshouse entrance on the right

Route 7

Knowle and Temple Balsall $5\frac{1}{2}$ miles

Start

From the parish church at Knowle (OS Sheet 139 GR 182767), or from Kixley Lane (see Route paragraph 1) – roadside parking and small lay-by.

Route

1. *With your back to the church, turn left to follow the minor road away from the village and go left into Kixley Lane. After about $\frac{1}{3}$ mile climb a stile on the left, and bear right to a stile in the hedge, then left along a curving field-edge to the Grand Union Canal.*

2. *Cross the high footbridge and follow the towpath left to a roadbridge. Turn right along the road and branch right into Waterfield Farm. Keeping ahead, pass through two sets of double-gates and follow a track between buildings. Becoming a hedged way, it runs along a broad ridge with good views on each side.*

3. *Turn through a gate to go left of Nappins Covert, continue right of a ruined brick barn to a gate, and bear left to a corner stile. Go over the next field diagonally to a gate/stile at the far corner and veer right to cross the River Blythe by a footbridge.*

4. *Turn left, cross a lane via stiles, and climb to a stile between trees. Go up past a barn to a stile on the left, from which a path leads into Barston churchyard. If making for the Bull's Head, take the road to the left for 100 yards.*

5. *Return to the barn and descend to a stile at the bottom right-hand corner of the field. Two more stiles lead to a house drive – there turn left. At a bend continue through a fieldgate and climb a stile on the right by a pool. Veering right to a stile in the facing hedge, turn sharp right to the far field corner, step through a wooden fence and go out to the junction of Hob Lane and Elvers Green Lane.*

6. *Turn left up Hob Lane to Piercil End, and fork left along a green lane to reach the B4101. (If conditions are too wet, return along Hob Lane and go left into Elvers Green Lane to reach the stile indicated in paragraph 8.) Turn right along the B4101 and first left to Temple Balsall. Here, take the path on the right (The Breadwalk) past the almshouses, church and Old Hall.*

7. *Cross a bridge and bear right through a kissing gate to a woodland path. Fork left to reach Temple Lane and turn right for a few yards to the B4101. Go left along it, passing a Warwickshire Wildlife Trust nature reserve and Springfield House (now a school). Leave the road at a left-hand bend, taking a path between holly bushes on the right.*

Continued on page 38

37

8. *Cross a drive to a stile and follow a right-hand hedge back to the B4101. Bear right along the road, and turn right into Elvers Green Lane. Go along the lane to a signposted gate on the left, just before Elvers Green Farm. Follow the left-hand field-edge to a stile and cross a little footbridge to the next stile. Ahead is a bridge over the Grand Union Canal, with Kixley Lane beyond.*

Access by bus
WMT local services from Solihull to Knowle.

Refreshments
The Bull's Head at Barston (food); teas at Almshouses, Temple Balsall, on summer Saturdays, Sundays and Bank Holidays.

The Almshouses, Temple Balsall

Berkswell and its Windmill

Outline
Berkswell – Baulk Lane – Carol Green – Catchems Corner – Berkswell Windmill – Berkswell Station – Ram Hall – Berkswell.

Summary
An easy circuit, mainly on waymarked fieldpaths, linking the attractive and interesting Berkswell village with Berkswell Windmill. If Berkswell Museum or the windmill are to be visited, the walk must be taken on a summer Sunday afternoon or a Bank Holiday. Allow about 20 minutes for the windmill, but much more for the church and museum.

Attractions
Berkswell village green is bordered on one side by cottages and a shop with Georgian bow windows, and by 19th century almshouses on the other. The old stocks always provoke comment. Why are there five leg holes, rather than six? No one knows, but it has been suggested that they were made for a one-legged lawbreaker and his two companions.

Facing the green are the gates of The Well House, a 17th century former rectory. It was the childhood home of Maud Watson, first winner of the Wimbledon Ladies' Tennis Championship in 1884, who is buried in the churchyard, near the porch. Left of the gates is the large well from which the village took its name. The monks who brought Christianity to the area used it to baptise converts. Beyond the well lie the almshouses' gardens, with access to Berkswell Village Museum. Run by volunteers, it has much interesting local information.

The parish church dates from the 12th century. Unusual features are a double crypt, possibly of Saxon origin, and a 16th century timber-framed priest's room over the porch. But how many mice can you count? There are eleven, the trade marks of woodcarver Robert Thompson.

In the churchyard look out for the broken pillar above the grave of James Owen, which symbolises the cutting off of his head in a gruesome sawmill accident in 1898, and that of James Weetman, who died in 1840 "of a broken heart". It was deliberately placed beside the path, so that the young lady who had trifled with his affections couldn't miss it. On another gravestone are carved 2 loaves, 21 eggs and 18 rashers of bacon – the deceased is said to have expired from overeating.

The Bear Inn has stood at the cross-roads for 400 years. Outside is a Russian cannon captured in 1855 by Captain Arthur Wilmot of Berkswell Hall.

Berkswell Windmill, built in 1826, is a typical Warwickshire tower mill on the site of a much earlier post mill. Its machinery and fittings are complete, though not in working order, but there are plenty of miller's tools to be seen and the sails are in place. The mill ground its last corn in 1948. It was restored in 1973.

Route 8

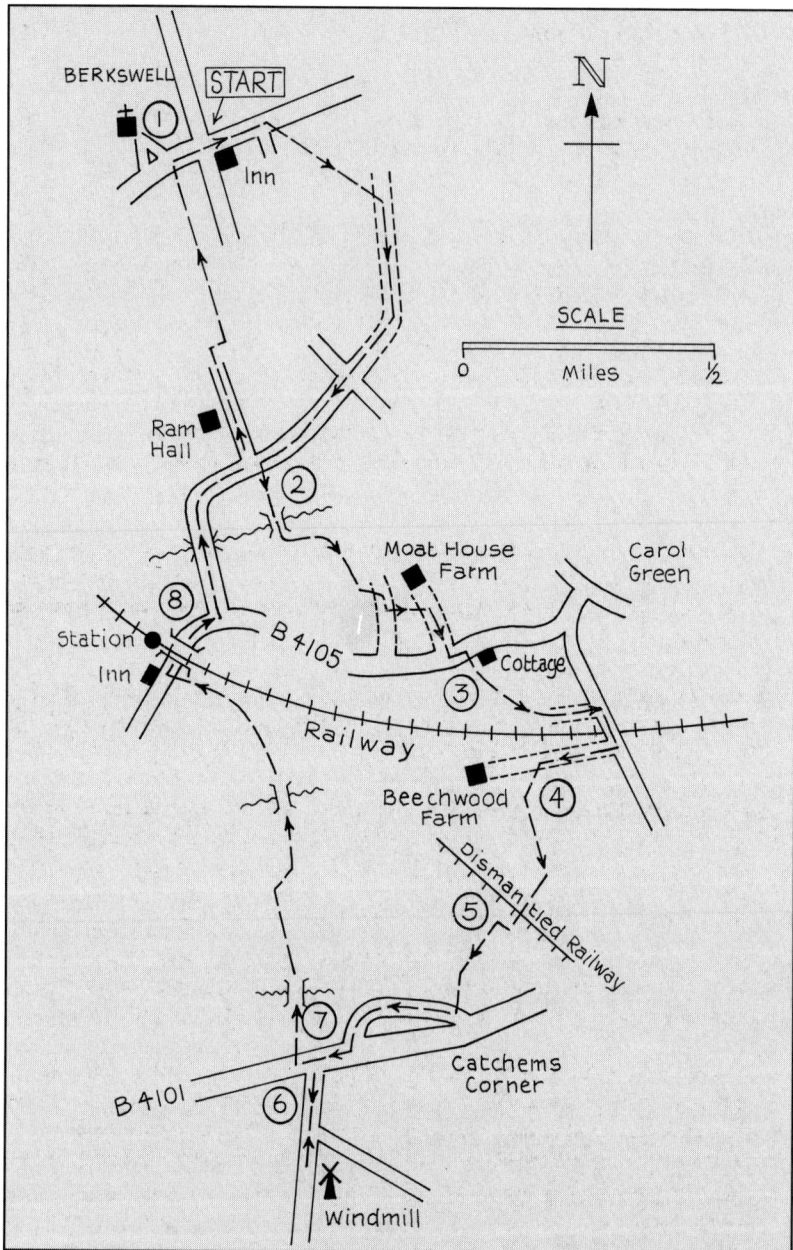

BERKSWELL START

N

① Inn

SCALE

0   Miles   ½

Ram Hall

②

Moat House Farm

Carol Green

⑧

Station Inn

B 4105

③ Cottage

Railway

Beechwood Farm ④

Dismantled Railway

⑤

Catchems Corner

⑦

B 4101 ⑥

Windmill

Route 8

Berkswell and its Windmill   5½ miles

Start
Roadside parking space in Meriden Road, Berkswell, or free public car-park near village green (OS Sheets 139 and 140 GR 246791).

Route

1. From the Bear Inn follow Coventry Road past Pound Close to a stile set back on the right. Go over a rise and between clumps of trees to a stile on a metalled drive. Turn right to Spencers Lane and cross to Baulk Lane.

2. Opposite the drive of Ram Hall turn left through a fieldgate and descend to a railed footbridge. Go left to the field-corner and swing right along the hedge to join a track leading to Moat House Farm. At a large oak, about 100 yards before the farm, cross diagonally right to a drive. Turn right for 50 yards to a stile on the left. Follow the ancient moat to a stile/gate, continue to a stile and turn right along a drive to the B4105.

3. Go left to Jasmine Cottage, and turn right along a path beside it. Continue over a stile and follow the left-hand field-edges past two more stiles to a railway cutting. From a stile/gate turn left along a track to a road, bear right over the railway and right again into the drive of Beechwood Farm.

4. Climb a stile on the left at the end of a hedge and cross to another at the far field corner. Bear left along a track to a stile/gate and follow the right-hand hedge through fields to a dismantled railway.

5. Turn right along the top of the embankment for a few steps and descend the far side. Follow the right-hand hedge to join a fenced path leading to Waste Lane at Catchems Corner, and turn right to the B4101. Go right and first left to visit Berkswell Windmill.

6. Return to the B4101 and bear left. Immediately beyond a bus shelter on the right, take a path beside the wall of a house to join a gravel drive. Keep ahead along a green track, climb a stile on the left, and turn right along a hedge to a stile.

7. Cross the stile and follow the waymarked path over a footbridge, then left of a hedge to a stile/gate. Bear right across a field to a stile in the opposite hedge and follow right-hand field-edges, via a footbridge, to a stile/gate on your right. In the next field turn left and keep on the same line as before, through two gateways, to the B4105, by Berkswell Station. To the left is the Railway Inn.

Continued on page 42

41

8. *Go under the railway, re-enter Baulk Lane on your left, and turn left along the drive to the Elizabethan Ram Hall. On the right, opposite the house, is a stile, cross it, turn left to a gate and descend to a stile/gate. Skirt anti-clockwise, climb a stile at the top right field corner and turn left to follow the far side of the hedge back to Berkswell.*

Access by train and bus
Trains to Berkswell Station (Birmingham New Street–Coventry line). Buses to Berkswell village (WMT Solihull–Coventry services).

Refreshments
The Bear Inn, Berkswell, and the Railway Inn by the station provide bar meals. Stores on B4101, near Berkswell Windmill. Teas on summer Sundays and Bank Holidays at the Reading Room, Meriden Road, Berkswell.

Kenilworth Castle

42

Kenilworth Castle and The Pleasance

Outline
Kenilworth Castle – Chase Wood – The Boot Inn – Honiley Church –
The Pleasance – Kenilworth Castle.

Summary
The walk mainly follows fieldpaths waymarked by Kenilworth Footpath Preserva-
tion Group, which also installed the railed footbridge crossed twice on the 6 mile
route. Walkers who prefer to visit Kenilworth Castle in the middle of their ramble,
rather than at the beginning or the end, can start from the lane between the Boot Inn
and Honiley Church (roadside parking, OS Sheet 139 GR 243722). Since the Castle
ruins are substantial, about two hours should be allowed for exploring them.

Attractions
Kenilworth Casle (maintained by English Heritage) was one of England's most
impressive buildings during the Middle Ages, and is an exciting place to visit today.
Enough of its red sandstone walls remain for us to imagine what it was like at its
peak in Queen Elizabeth I's time, when held by her favourite, Robert Dudley, Earl
of Leicester. The last of the Queen's three visits there, in 1575, forms the basis of Sir
Walter Scott's novel *Kenilworth*.

Visitors enter the site along a causeway from the south car-park. Known as the
Tiltyard, it was used for jousting in the late Middle Ages. Imagine how pairs of
knights, with lances dressed (*i.e.* at the ready), would have galloped along it, one on
either side of a barrier, each determined to unseat the other.

The main buildings within the Castle walls are the massive Keep, begun in the
12th century, and John of Gaunt's Great Hall, built two hundred years later. There
are also many lesser ones, including Leicester's Gatehouse and Stables, which house
an information display and the English Heritage shop.

In 1265 the Battle of Kenilworth took place, when Edward, son of Henry III,
defeated Simon de Montfort the Younger, before going on to beat Simon the Elder
at Evesham. In the following year many surviving de Montfort supporters endured
a six months' siege at the Castle, before surrendering to the King. In those days,
before gunpowder was introduced to Europe, such a mighty fortress was
impregnable and its defenders could only be starved out.

After being occupied by Parliamentarian troops during the Civil War,
Kenilworth Castle was partly demolished in the 1650s.

To the west of the Castle lay a great Mere. It was expanded during the reign of
King John and its northern arm filled the dip in Purlieu Lane (the name of which
suggests that it marked an ancient boundary). The Mere was drained in 1650.

Further along our walk, Chase Lane and Chase Wood were named from a 19th
century steeplechase.

Continued on page 46

Route 9

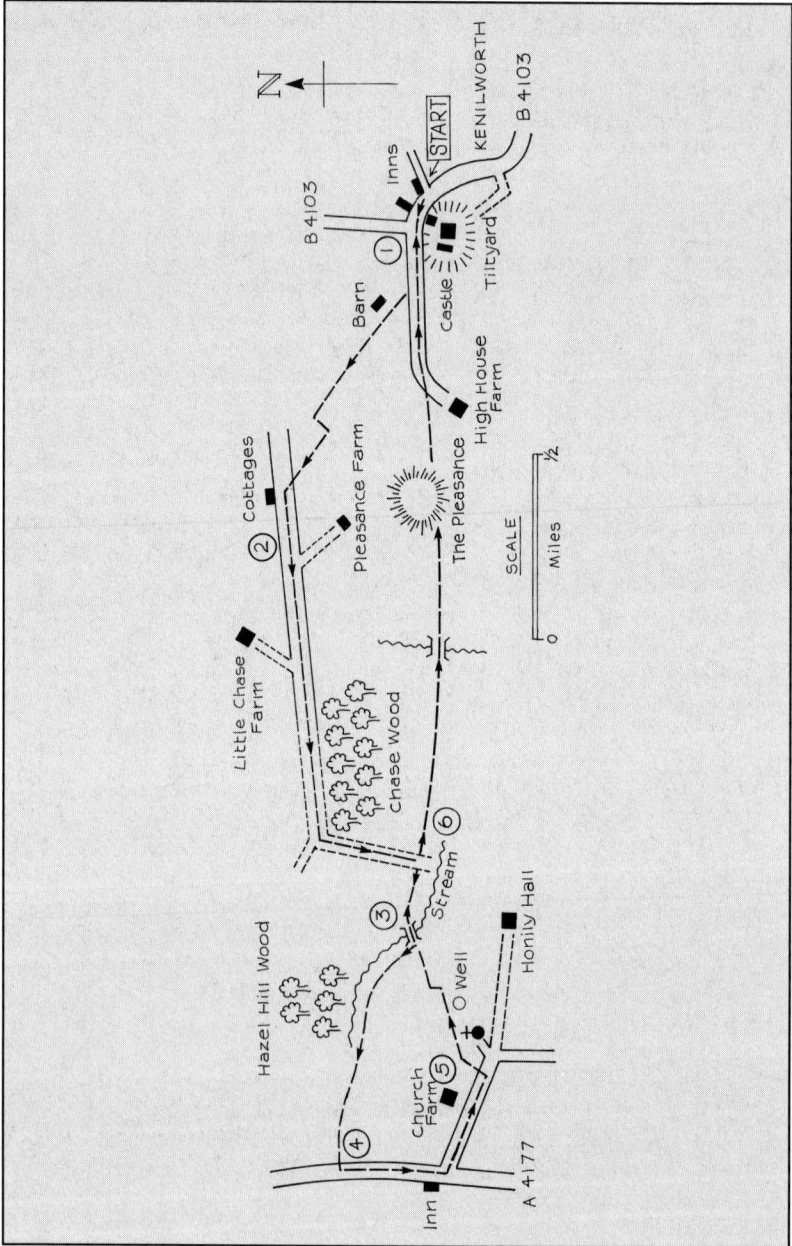

Route 9

Kenilworth Castle and The Pleasance

4 miles or 6 miles

Start

    Free car-park opposite Castle Green on the B4103 (OS Sheet 140 GR 279724; for the 6 mile route OS Sheet 139 is also required).

Route

1. *From the car-park follow the embankment between the road and the dry moat, and descend to the unsurfaced Purlieu Lane. After about 200 yards climb a stile on the right and ascend to a gate at the far field corner, beyond a brick barn. Go half-left across the next field to a stile, from which the path runs to the far corner of a third field. From an exit stile, follow the right-hand hedge to a stile, and cross to a stile on Chase Lane, opposite cottages.*

2. *Bear left along the lane and continue beside Chase Wood. At the end of the wood turn left, down a broad track at the edge of a long field. (On reaching a path junction at the bottom of the field, choose between a 4 mile and a 6 mile ramble. **For the shorter walk,** go left, as described in 6 below. For the longer route, which returns to this point, turn right along a field-margin.)*

3. *At the end of the field cross a railed footbridge and bear right, beside Hazel Hill Wood. At the corner take the hedge-gap ahead and follow the right-hand field-edge past a grove of trees. Cross to a marker post where the hedge on the right ends, and go over the next field to a gap beside a tree bearing a direction arrow.*

4. *Turn left along the grassy margin of the A4177 to the Honiley Boot Inn, and take the lane opposite. After about ⅓-mile cross a stile on the left (but first, you may like to continue for 200 yards to see the charming little 18th century Honiley Church).*

5. *From the stile cross to a gap beside a tree stump, and follow a hedge to a waymarked gap on the right. Continue beside another hedge, beyond which is the ancient St John's Well. Descend to a marker post, bear right along a field-edge to the footbridge used earlier, and retrace your steps to the track from Chase Wood, which you previously descended.*

6. *Cross the track and continue down two long field-edges to a railed footbridge. Follow the hedge on the left to a stile, then a hedge on the right to the next stile, and cross the right-hand edge of The Pleasance to a stile. Finally, an enclosed path leads past High House Farm to Purlieu Lane, with its impressive view of the Castle.*

Towards the end of the ramble we pass the site of The Pleasance. It dates from 1414, when Henry V cleared and drained part of the Mere in order to lay out a timber-framed summer house and garden. Two diamond-shaped moats, one within the other, can be seen in the field. Originally they were linked to the Mere by a wide channel, along which boats could approach from the Castle.

Refreshments
Inns at Castle Green, Kenilworth, and at Honiley; shop (pop, ice-cream) at Castle Green; ice-cream at Kenilworth Castle.

Access by bus
Midland Red South services, connecting Coventry, Kenilworth, Leamington Spa, Warwick and Stratford upon Avon, pass Kenilworth Castle.

Stoneleigh Church

Romans and Countrymen: Stoneleigh and Baginton

Outline
Stoneleigh – River Sowe – Baginton Church – Lunt Roman Fort – Baginton village – Stoneleigh.

Summary
Fieldpath walking beside the little River Sowe, from Stoneleigh to Baginton, returning by quiet lanes. Stoneleigh is a lovely old village, and at Baginton there is a rather quaint church and a reconstructed Roman fort. Aerial activity from Coventry Airport will be of interest , and there may be time to include a visit to the Midland Air Museum at Baginton.

Attractions
At Stoneleigh (originally Stanlei) we pass through riverside meadows and between old houses, including The Cruck Cottage of ancient timber construction, to reach the 700 years-old church. Note the filled-in Norman arch outside the north wall. In the church, which has one of England's finest Norman chancel arches, you can buy an informative guide to the village. The meadows around the church are preserved by a charitable trust. Passing the magnificent gabled Manor Farmhouse in Vicarage Road, we reach The Green, where stand mellow stone almshouses of 1594 and a still-active smithy dated 1851.

Stoneleigh is on the 100-mile Centenary Way walking route, established by the county council to commemorate its hundredth anniversary in 1989. Nearby stands the great Stoneleigh Abbey, its architecture ranging back from the 18th century to early monastic buildings 500 years older. The grounds now house the National Agricultural Centre, where the Royal Agricultural Show is held annually in July.

A pleasant walk through the Sowe valley leads to another old village, Baginton. It entered history briefly one morning in September 1398, when Henry Bolingbroke, Duke of Hereford, rode out from its castle to Gosford Green, now part of Coventry. There, as powerfully portrayed in Shakespeare's *Richard II*, he had a dramatic confrontation with Thomas Mowbray, Duke of Norfolk, when each accused the other of treason. Both were banished by the king, but Bolingbroke returned the following year, forced Richard to surrender and began his reign as Henry IV.

Baginton Castle was then the home of Sir William Bagot, one of the "creatures" (Shakespeare's word) of King Richard. Now a scanty ruin, it lies amid undergrowth next to the rather curious church, which contains fine brasses of Sir William and his lady. In the churchyard are the graves of seven young wartime Polish airmen, who crashed nearby in 1940.

But Baginton has older memories. Lunt Roman Fort dates from about AD60, when Queen Boudica was fighting the new Roman rulers. Its ground-plan can be

Continued on page 50

Route 10

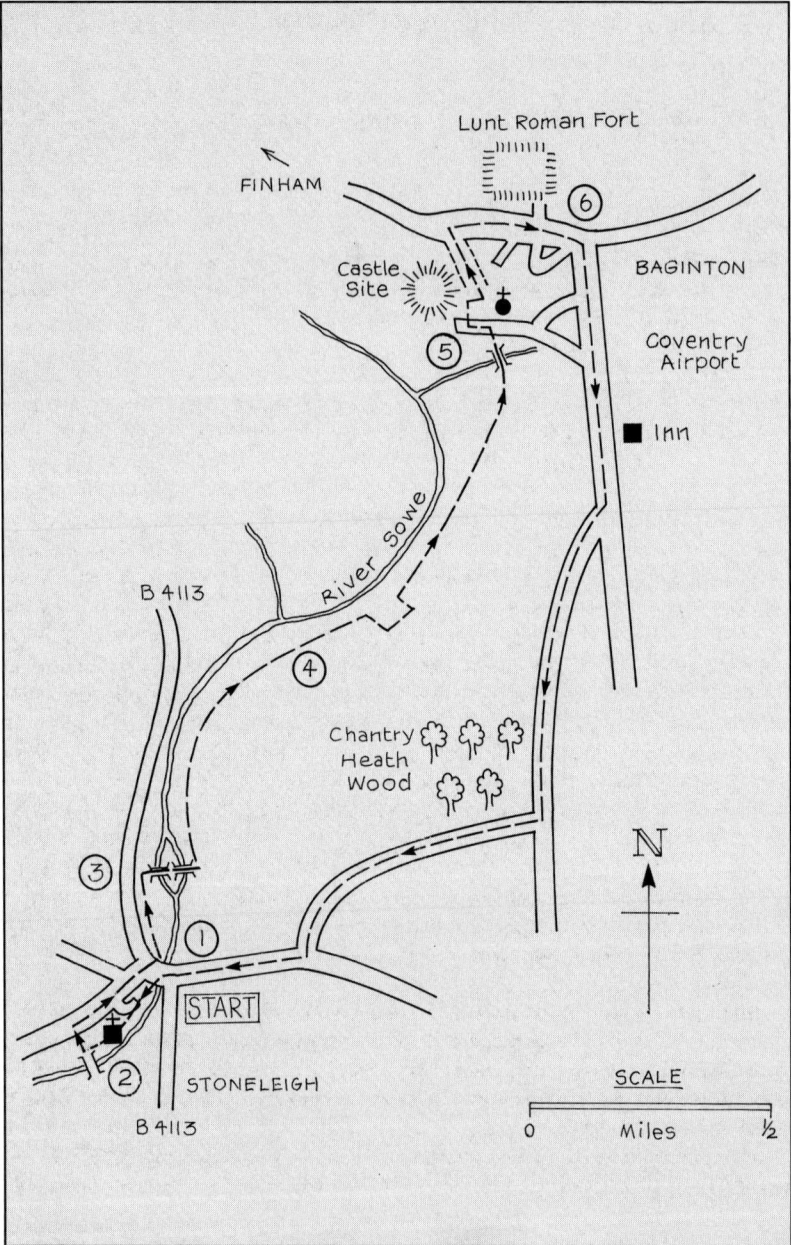

Lunt Roman Fort

FINHAM

Castle Site

BAGINTON

⑥

Coventry Airport

⑤

■ Inn

River Sowe

B 4113

④

Chantry Heath Wood

N

③

①

START

② STONELEIGH

B 4113

SCALE

0   Miles   ½

Route 10

Romans and Countrymen: Stoneleigh and Baginton   5 miles

Start

Off-road parking at Stoneleigh (or Rennie) Bridge on B4113 (formerly A444) (OS Sheet 140 GR 333727).

Route

1. Cross the River Sowe by the bridge and turn left through a gate to a riverside meadow. Follow the right-hand hedge to a gate and take the road ahead, between cottages, to Stoneleigh churchyard.

2. Pass through to the far gate, from which a path descends a meadow to a footbridge over the river. Do not cross, but turn right up a drive and right again along Vicarage Road into the village. Continue past The Green to Coventry Road (B4113) and bear left along the footpath beside it.

3. After 300 yards, turn right down a signed path from a gate, passing a small brick building. Cross the divided River Sowe by two bridges to reach a meadow, and turn left to a stile/gate. Follow the hedge on your right and, towards the far end of the field, change sides of it at a stile.

4. Continue to a corner stile and along a narrow field, then skirt a sewage farm fence to a stile by a large, sawn-off tree-trunk. Descend to the left and go right along the bottom of the field. After four more stiles, the path climbs gently to a stile near a gate. Beyond, cross a footbridge and kissing gate near Pool Cottage, and climb to emerge on a lane, opposite Baginton Church.

5. Turn left, and take an arrowed path on the right through the churchyard. A gate leads out to the overgrown site of Baginton Castle. There, turn right along a path to another churchyard gate and bear left, following a path through the overgrown area to a gateway in a tall wooden fence. Keep ahead along a track past a house to a road, Mill Hill, and turn right to Lunt Roman Fort.

6. Leaving the fort, continue along the main road (here called Coventry Road). Follow it through a junction, where it swings right to pass the Oak Inn and Coventry Airport. Fork right, and at the next junction, by Chantry Heath Wood, bear right again down a pleasant by-way ending at a T-junction. Stoneleigh Bridge lies downhill, to the right.

49

clearly seen, some of the timber buildings were reconstructed by the Royal Engineers in 1971 and there is an interesting museum. The fort is unique in having a *gyrus*, or cavalry training ring. It is believed to have been the main centre for breaking and training horses seized from the Iceni tribe after Boudica's defeat.

Refreshments
The Oak Inn (bar meals), or Coventry Airport Cafe, both at Baginton. None at Stoneleigh.

Access by bus
WMT service: Coventry–Finham ($\frac{1}{2}$ mile from Baginton). Heyfordian Coaches, Banbury: Kenilworth–Stoneleigh service.

The Green, Stoneleigh

Coombe Abbey and its Bridleways

Outline
Coombe Abbey Country Park – Twelve O'clock Ride – Birchley Wood –
Coombe Abbey Country Park.

Summary
A short walk of about $1\frac{1}{2}$ miles on good paths within Coombe Abbey Country Park,
with the option of a second circuit of about 4 miles on clear bridleways outside the
park. Some of the walking is on Warwickshire County Council's Centenary Way
long-distance footpath.

Attractions
If the Gunpowder Plot of 1605 had been the roaring success that Guy Fawkes and
his fellow conspirators prayed for, they would probably have replaced James I by
his eldest daughter, Princess Elizabeth. The princess, who was then living at
Coombe Abbey, later became "the Winter Queen" of Bohemia, after marrying
Frederick, Elector of the Palatine.

Today the Abbey, just outside Coventry's eastern boundary, is the centre of a
country park opened in 1966 and run by the city's Leisure Services. In earlier times it
was a Cistercian monastery, founded in 1150, and later became the seat of the Earls
of Craven until 1923. The grounds were landscaped by the famous Capability
Brown about 1770 and the country park occupies 280 acres of them, mainly
woodland. A long, narrow lake – said to be the largest natural lake in Warwickshire – creates a fine vista from the house.

After crossing the stone bridge over the moat, look for a plaque on the building
to the left giving a short history of the Abbey. Above arches to the right is a large
sun-dial, and within them a notice indicates the period of each part of the building,
the earliest being of Norman origin.

Among the buildings is a children's indoor play area and in the park there is an
adventure playground. Look for the permanent exhibition and audio-visual display
by the Rangers' Office, from which we learn that in 1823 the Coombe Estate
contained 2,519 acres of workable land, 1,259 acres of woods, 32 acres of lanes and
20 acres of canal. Other attractions include the Fishery, open daily during the
fishing season, the 15-acre Victorian Garden and a Children's Boating Lake for
under 14s, open in summer. There are also boat trips on the main lake. *Discover
Coombe*, a leaflet available from the Rangers' Office, includes a good map of the
country park and is useful for the $1\frac{1}{2}$ mile walk.

Refreshments   Food and drinks available at Coombe Abbey.

Route 11

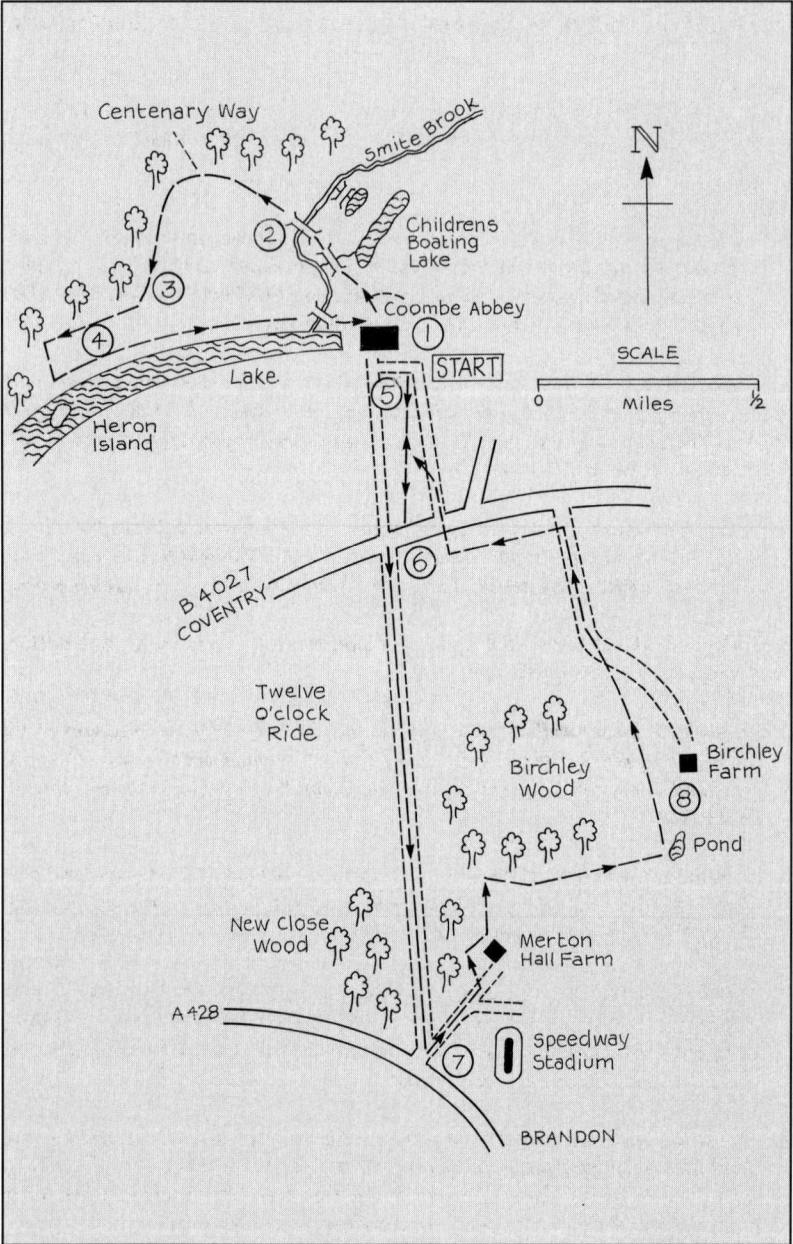

Centenary Way

Smite Brook

Childrens Boating Lake

Coombe Abbey

START

② ③ ④ ⑤ ① ⑥ ⑦ ⑧

Lake

Heron Island

N

SCALE

0   Miles   ½

B 4027 COVENTRY

Twelve O'clock Ride

Birchley Wood

Birchley Farm

Pond

New Close Wood

Merton Hall Farm

A 428

Speedway Stadium

BRANDON

52

Route 11

Coombe Abbey and its Bridleways $1\frac{1}{2}$ miles or $5\frac{1}{2}$ miles

Start
Pay car-park at Coombe Abbey Country Park, 5 miles east of Coventry (OS Sheet 140 GR 404797), or roadside at south end of Twelve O'clock Ride (GR 405773).

Route
1. *From the car-park, cross the bridge over the moat and pass under the arch. Continue past the Abbey buildings to a 4-way junction and bear left through a metal gate. Following the pointer indicating Wrautums Field and the Adventure Play Area, cross the bridge by the Children's Boating Lake.*

2. *Beyond the next bridge, follow a Centenary Way marker along a path to the right. At a junction fork left, still on the Centenary Way, but where the Way forks right to leave the country park, go left through scattered woodland and cross Little Wrautums Field, passing log seats.*

3. *At a T-junction of paths in the trees beyond, turn right. The path swings right to skirt the inside edge of the park, passing a Site of Special Scientific Interest on your left. Bearing left, it reaches the Lake, where there is a hide for observing birds.*

4. *Follow a path to the left alongside the Lake, crossing a footbridge and walking through the gardens to the Abbey.*

5. **To start the longer walk,** *return to the car-park. Leave it via a fence-gap on the south side to reach a picnic area, beyond which another fence-gap leads out to grassland. Walk parallel to the drive on your right, before crossing to the main gate on the B4027.*

6. *Opposite is the Twelve O'clock Ride, a straight north to south fenced bridleway used by the Centenary Way. Follow it between fields to a gate, then through New Close Wood to a track junction at the far side.*

7. *Turn left, leaving the Centenary Way, and, just before Merton Hall Farm, go left through a waymarked gate. Bear right in the field, skirting woodland, to a kissing gate. Turn left along the edge of the wood to a corner, then right beside Birchley Wood to a gate at its south-east corner.*

8. *Follow the bridleway through the corner of the wood to an exit gate and turn left along its edge, joining the surfaced drive of Birchley Farm. At the B4027, walk the side-verges to the left, passing a road junction, and re-enter the country park at its first gate on the right. Veer left across the grass back to the car-park.*

53

Access by bus
WMT 13C service Coventry–Coombe Abbey (summer and special events).
Midland Red 86 (Coventry–Rugby) follows A428 south of New Close Wood.

No expense spared – Leigh monument in St Mary's Church, Stoneleigh

Clowes Wood and Earlswood Lakes

Outline
Clowes Wood – Earlswood Lakes – Salter Street – Lady Lane –
Earlswood Lakes – Clowes Wood.

Summary
The 4 mile walk is on footpaths through Clowes Wood and beside the lovely
Earlswood Lakes. The $2\frac{1}{2}$ mile extension, which mainly follows quiet lanes, passes
near three inns and a village store. Much of the Stratford upon Avon Canal towpath
north of Lapworth has been virtually unwalkable for years, but British Waterways
is in process of opening it up as a walkway from Birmingham to Stratford.
Therefore, walkers using this route may one day find the towpath worth
investigating as an agreeable short cut between Salter Street (B4102) and Lady
Lane. The lakeside paths are also eroded and often muddy – boots or wellies
recommended.

Attractions
The 73 acres of Clowes Wood, together with the adjoining New Fallings Coppice
and Earlswood Lakes, form a Site of Special Scientific Interest. Since 1974 the wood
has been owned and managed as a nature reserve by Warwickshire Wildlife Trust.
Oak, birch, beech, alder and rowan are the main trees found there. Since the ground
is acidic and very wet underfoot in places, it is advisable to keep to the route
described. The nature reserve includes heathland and a 200 years-old hay meadow.

Nearly two centuries after they were constructed, Earlswood Lakes have
become almost natural features of the landscape. Bordered by trees and footpaths
and divided by causeways, the three reservoirs were built in 1810 to supply water to
the Stratford upon Avon Canal. The cost to the canal company of the 51 acres of
Earlswood Common, out of which the great pools were cut, was a mere £969 8s 9d.
Though the Act of Parliament authorising the local canal was passed in 1793, the
company met problems in raising the money for its construction, and the waterway
was not fully opened until 1816. Within twenty years it was feeling the pinch from
the new-fangled railways, and was sold to the Great Western Railway in 1856. Like
most canals, the Stratford upon Avon suffered a long decline until the second half of
the 20th century, when tourist traffic brought a revival.

The original Salter Street Chapel was built in 1840, largely from the money paid
thirty years earlier for the land occupied by the lakes. Its tower was added in 1861
and the rest of the building reconstructed in 1899.

Bedsworth Farm, north of the chapel, was formerly a manor house and is
known to have had its own chapel in 1729.

Route 12

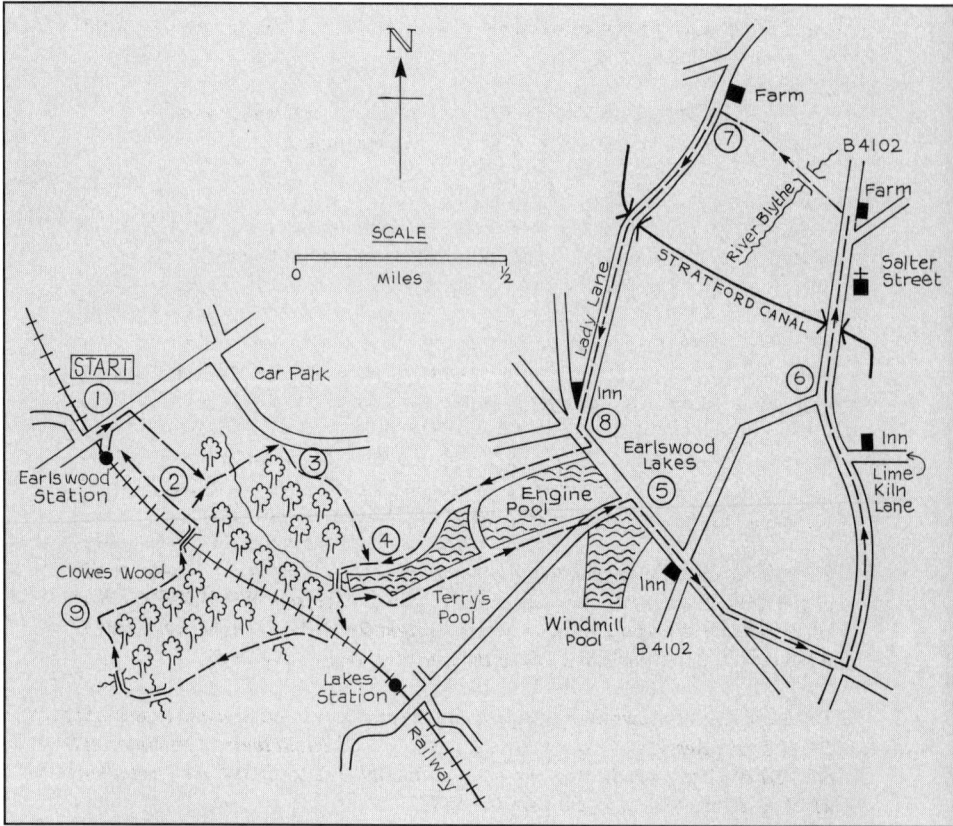

Map labels

N

SCALE

0 — Miles — ½

START
①
Earlswood
Station

Car Park

②

③

Clowes Wood

⑨

④

Engine
Pool

Terry's
Pool

Lakes
Station

Railway

Windmill
Pool

B 4102

⑧
Inn

Earlswood
Lakes
⑤

Inn

⑥

Lady Lane

STRATFORD CANAL

River Blythe

⑦

Farm

B 4102

Farm

Salter
Street

Inn

Lime
Kiln
Lane

Earlswood Lakes

Route 12

Clowes Wood and Earlswood Lakes

4 miles or $6\frac{1}{2}$ miles

Start

From Earlswood Station (OS Sheet 139 GR 095743), or from Clowes Wood car-park (free) in Wood Lane (GR 102743 – see paragraph 2).

Route

1. *Leaving the station, turn right along the road and take an enclosed path on the right, signed "Clowes Wood". Pass an old moat on your left, enter the wood at a stile, and keep ahead along a path.*

2. *Fork right, go through a clearing and cross a little brook. Follow the main path, keeping near the left-hand edge of the wood and swinging right to the Wood Lane entrance (the motorists' starting point for the walk).*

3. *Step over a wooden fence ahead, and descend to the right alongside the wood (here known as New Fallings Coppice), re-entering it right of a timber building. The path continues through to Terry's Pool, one of the three Earlswood Lakes.*

4. *Walk anti-clockwise round the pool. Pass the causeway, and continue beside Engine Pool. On reaching the road dividing Engine Pool from Windmill Pool, bear left to the dam.* **Choose now between turning right for the longer walk or left for the shorter one** *(see paragraph 8 where the routes rejoin).*

5. *The longer walk follows the narrow road to the right along the dam and crosses the B4102 by the Reservoir Inn and the village stores. Fork left at the next junction, and turn left at a cross-roads. After $\frac{1}{2}$ mile pass the end of Lime Kiln Lane (just along which is the Bull's Head) and join the B4102.*

6. *Turn right and follow it over the Stratford upon Avon Canal and past Salter Street Chapel. Beyond a road junction is a signed path from a stile on the left, opposite Bedsworth Farm. Climb the stile and go down a field to a stile/gate, cross the young River Blythe via a concrete culvert and continue to another stile. Beyond it, follow the hedge on your right, via a stile/gate, to a gate on Lady Lane.*

7. *Turn left, recrossing the canal and passing the Red Lion. Bear left at a cross-roads to return to Engine Pool, noting a feeder canal.*

8. *Rejoining the shorter route, bear right of Engine Pool to return to Terry's Pool. After passing the point where you emerged earlier from the woods, turn right over a footbridge and stiles. Cross the railway embankment and follow the waymarked*

Continued on page 58

path skirting Clowes Wood. Beyond the third footbridge, at a corner of the wood, the path is arrowed to a stile, then across a field to the next stile. After crossing this, turn right to a stile/gate leading into the wood.

9. *Though the right-of-way runs outside the wood, there is a concessionary path through – both lead to a footbridge over the railway. Having crossed, to return to the station go sharp left along a path running parallel to the line. Otherwise, keep ahead along a field-edge to reach the stile into the wood and continue to the Wood Lane car-park, as described in paragraph 2.*

Access by train
Earlswood Station (Birmingham Snow Hill to Stratford upon Avon line).

Refreshments
The Reservoir Inn and the nearby village stores, the Bull's Head (children's playground) and the Red Lion are all on or near the longer route.

Earlswood Lakes

58

Henley's Castle Mount

Outline
Henley in Arden – The Mount – Preston Field Lane – Preston Bagot – Stratford upon Avon Canal – Pettiford Lane – River Alne – Blackford Mill – Henley in Arden.

Summary
Fieldpaths, an old unsurfaced lane, a canal towpath and a riverside path, plus a few short connecting stretches of road make up this varied ramble. The terrain is equally divided between the hilly landscape (by Warwickshire standards) north-east of Henley in Arden and the level walking beside the Stratford upon Avon Canal and the River Alne. Part of the ramble follows the waymarked Heart of England Way, a 100-mile walking route from Cannock Chase to the Cotswolds.

Attractions
This is real "king of the castle" country, for just outside Henley in Arden rises The Mount, on which stood the castle of the powerful de Montfort family. Not a stone remains, but it is easy to imagine how Thurstan de Montfort, at the end of the 11th century, saw its military possibilities. In the castle's first years there was no town below – just the huddled village of Beaudesert ("beautiful wilderness" in the Norman French spoken by those early nobles). But after the granting of a charter in 1140 for a weekly fair and market, Henley began to grow. Its prosperity came to an end in 1265, when the Lord of the Manor, Peter de Montfort, sided with his cousin Simon against Henry III's troops at the Battle of Evesham. The battle was lost and both were killed. The reprisals included partial destruction of the castle.

Henley's other attractions include two old churches standing only 200 yards apart at each end of Beaudesert Lane, the nearby Guild Hall and a 500 years-old broken market cross on High Street, plus many picturesque buildings and the town's most famous product – ice-cream. Though St John's Church at Henley dates – like the Guild Hall – from the mid-15th century, St Nicholas's at Beaudesert is 300 years older.

Along the Stratford upon Avon Canal towpath note the split bridges, built in two halves with a one inch gap between, so that the towropes could pass through without the horses being unhitched.

Buildings of interest include the little Norman hilltop church and the Manor House at Preston Bagot, and Blackford Mill on the River Alne. It is worth stepping into the churchyard for its extensive views. The lovely gabled and half-timbered Manor House, by the B4095, has been converted to apartments. Blackford Mill stands on an ancient mill site. There is a possible reference to it as early as 1296 and the building continued in use as a mill until 1957. It is now a private house, its 15ft waterwheel hidden within brick casing.

Route 13

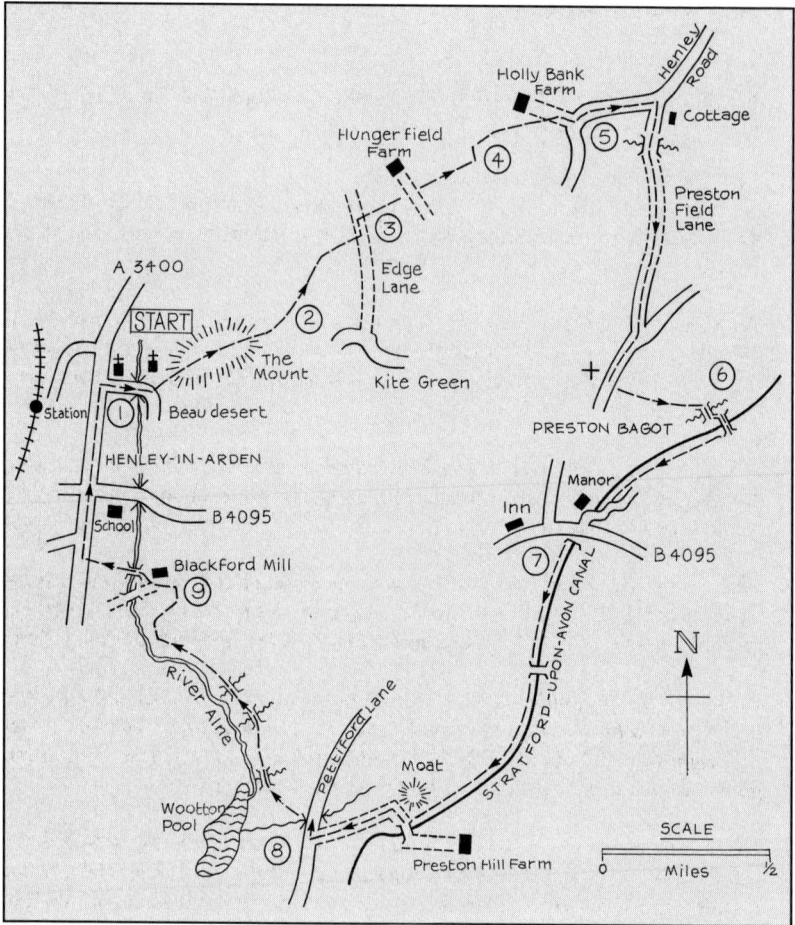

Route 13

Henley's Castle Mount

7 miles

Start

Beaudesert Lane, Henley in Arden (OS Sheet 151 GR 151660). Roadside parking in High Street and Beaudesert Lane.

Route

1. *From St John's Church in High Street turn along Beaudesert Lane, passing St Nicholas's Church. Go through a kissing gate, climb the steep path over The Mount and bear left up to three stiles at a field corner.*

2. *Take the left-hand stile (marked "Heart of England Way", which you follow to Henley Road – paragraph 4) along a green track for 400 yards to a stile on the right. Cross a field to a stile, and turn left along Edge Lane, now just a narrow hedged path.*

3. *Turn off right at a stile and, aiming between tall trees, cross a field and the drive of Hungerfield Farm. Descend right of a hedge and, when it bears away, keep ahead to a stile leading into a copse.*

4. *Pass through the copse, climb to a stile in the upper hedge and continue over a rise to a stile right of a line of tall cypresses at Holly Bank Farm. Climb a second stile and go down the field to join the farm drive at a gate, following it out to Henley Road.*

5. *Go left for nearly $\frac{1}{3}$ mile, and turn right into the unsurfaced Preston Field Lane, which, from a bend, angles back past a cottage. Continue to a road junction and bear right to a stile opposite Preston Bagot church. Descend the field to a gate and go down a long, sloping field to a stile/gate at the bottom.*

6. *Cross a stream by a railed footbridge, and follow a fenced path to a split-bridge on the Stratford upon Avon Canal. Go over it and take the towpath to the right. Where it ends, beyond the Haven Tea Rooms, cross a lane to resume towpath walking under the B4095 to another split-bridge. The Manor House stands nearby and the Crab Mill Inn lies just along the road to Henley.*

7. *Keep to the towpath for over a mile. At the second bridge, follow the drive of Preston Hill Farm to the right to reach Pettiford Lane. (Where the drive bends, look for an ancient moat on the right.)*

8. *Turn right over Pettiford Bridge to a stile/gate on the left. Cross to a little footbridge at the far right corner of a vast meadow and follow the River Alne upstream to Blackford Mill.*

Continued on page 62

61

9. *Bear left beside the mill and right at the end of it. Go over a railed bridge and follow a fenced path to a stile leading to Henley High School's playing fields. Cross to a stile on the A3400 and turn right into the town.*

Access by train and bus
Train to Henley in Arden (Birmingham Snow Hill–Stratford upon Avon line). Midland Red South Birmingham–Stratford upon Avon services.

Refreshments
The Crab Mill Inn and the Haven Tea Rooms at Preston Bagot; inns, cafes and ice-cream at Henley in Arden.

St John's Church, High Street, Henley in Arden

Warwick: Castle, Canal and Countryside

Outline
Warwick Race Course – Grand Union Canal – Hatton – Wedgnock
Old Park – Warwick

Summary
Easy walking across the Race Course and along the Grand Union Canal towpath to
Hatton, then on good tracks and bridleways to join a farm road with a distant
prospect of Warwick, before descending to the town.

Attractions
There is so much to see in Warwick that, if time is to be found for a ramble, a choice
has to be made. A good idea is to visit the Castle in the morning and to walk in the
afternoon. Allow over two hours for the Castle buildings, plus time for exploring
the grounds.

Warwick Castle grew over many centuries, beginning with the Mound raised in
914 by Ethelfleda, daughter of King Alfred, and achieving its present impressive
appearance in the late 18th century. In 1978 the Castle was sold by the Earl of
Warwick to Madame Tussaud's.

As a military fortress its defences were rarely put to the test, though in 1264,
during the Barons' War against Henry III, the north wall was smashed in and the
Earl and Countess captured, and in 1642 the Castle survived a two weeks' siege by
Royalists. A serious fire occurred in 1871, when the Private Apartments and Great
Hall were damaged.

We enter the Courtyard by the Gate House and find the Armoury to our left.
The weapons and suits of armour on display are fascinating, as are the battlements,
a walk along which involves climbing and descending some 200 steps.

Overlooking the River Avon are the Private Apartments and State Rooms, built
in sumptuous style during the 17th and 18th centuries. Madame Tussaud's has
peopled the Apartments with realistic wax figures representing a weekend party in
1898, when the guests included the Prince of Wales (later King Edward VII) and
young Winston Churchill.

The Dungeon and the Torture Chamber, though very interesting, are not to
everyone's taste, nor is the Watergate (or Ghost) Tower. A tape relates how Sir
Fulke Greville was murdered there by a manservant in 1628. He is said to haunt the
room to this day.

Warwick Racecourse is also known as Lammas Field. Lammas, the first day of
August, was formerly a harvest festival. Certain lands normally used for growing
crops were then opened for common pasture and other purposes.

The canal we follow was originally the Warwick & Birmingham. An information board at Hatton Bottom Lock outlines its history. Opened in 1800, it
Continued on page 66

Route 14

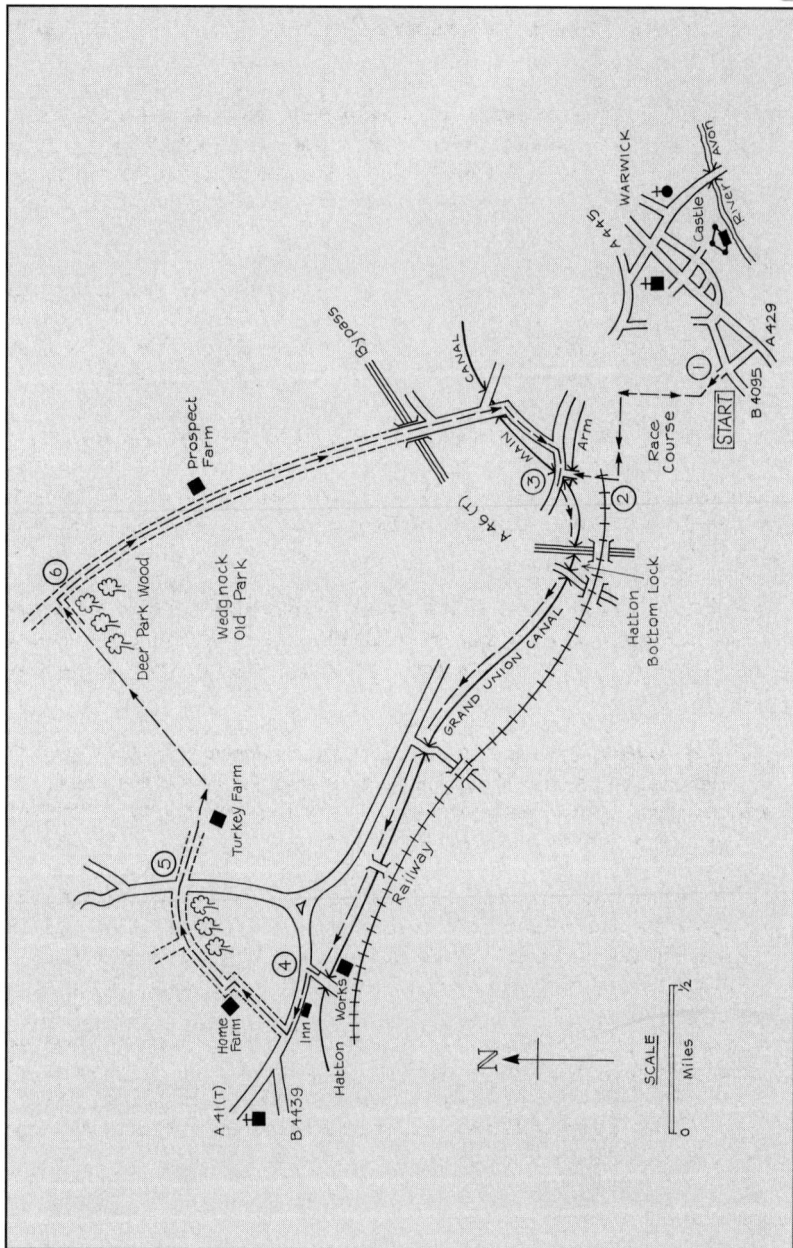

Route 14

Warwick: Castle, Canal and Countryside   6 miles

Start

> Free car-park at Warwick Race Course, off B4095 (OS Sheet 151 GR 277647).
> Alternatively Saltisford Canal Trust car-park, off A425 (GR 271656), Hatton
> Bottom Lock picnic area (GR 266655) or pay car-park at Hatton (GR 243669).

Route

1. *From the public car-park within the main entrance of Warwick Race Course, go
through a gap in the course railings to a direction post and take the path that climbs
diagonally right towards two large oaks. Walk right of a line of trees to the north
side of the course and follow the outside of the white railings to the left.*

2. *At the turn, bear sharp right, leave the course by ducking under a fence at a corner,
climb a stile and ascend to the right to reach a stile above railway lines. Cross
carefully, follow a fenced path between factories and go over the Saltisford Arm of
the Grand Union Canal (passing the Saltisford Canal Trust car-park) to the A425
Birmingham Road.*

3. *Bear left over the main canal and descend, right, to the towpath. Follow it under the
bridge and soon under the Bypass – A46(T) – to Hatton Bottom Lock, and
continue for $1\frac{3}{4}$ miles to the car-park and British Waterways' Workshops at
Hatton.*

4. *Turn right to the A41(T) and left along its footpath. Pass the Waterman Inn and
bear right onto the surfaced drive of Home Farm. Turn left beside the outbuildings
and left again beyond them, then right through double-gates to a track running left
of woods. At a track junction fork right to a lane.*

5. *Go right for a few yards and take a track on the left to Turkey Farm. From a gate,
skirt left of the farm buildings and pass a pond to enter a sloping field. Turn left and
follow the bridleway alongside a hedge, first on the right of it, then on the left. Go
through a gate and take the track past Deer Park Wood to a metalled drive.*

6. *Turn right for $\frac{1}{2}$ mile to Prospect Farm (the prospect is of Warwick, dominated by
the tall, slim tower of St Mary's Church) and, in another $\frac{1}{2}$ mile or so, cross the A46
Bypass bridge. Just beyond, bear right at a junction and continue to the A425. Turn
right, then left over the Saltisford Arm of the canal, and retrace your steps back
across the Race Course to the car-park.*

amalgamated with others to form the Grand Union Canal Company in 1929. A great modernisation scheme begun in 1932 was never completed, because the government grant proved inadequate, but disused original locks can be seen beside their 1930s replacements at the Bottom Lock and at some of the other 21 locks that raise the canal 150 feet out of the Avon valley.

Towards the end of the walk we reach Prospect Farm in Wedgnock Old Park (now farmland) and enjoy a fine view of Warwick, crowned by the tower of the Collegiate Church of St Mary.

Refreshments
Inns and cafes in Warwick; restaurants and cafe at Castle; inn at Hatton; picnic site at Hatton Bottom Lock.

Access by train or bus
Train to Warwick (Birmingham–Leamington Spa line). Midland Red South services from Coventry, Kenilworth, Leamington Spa and Stratford upon Avon.

Ducks on the green at Radway (Route 16)

Stratford Shire Horse Centre

Outline
Shire Horse Centre – Clifford Chambers – Cold Comfort Farm – Atherstone
Hill Farm – Preston on Stour – Alscot Park – Atherstone on Stour –
Clifford Chambers – Shire Horse Centre.

Summary
This varied walk near Stratford upon Avon includes an easy hill climb, giving lovely
views of the Cotswolds, three attractive villages and the grounds of a stately home.
From the Shire Horse Centre we follow fieldpaths to Clifford Chambers and climb a
gentle hill. A lane leads to Preston on Stour, where a path descends through Alscot
Park to Atherstone on Stour. Returning to Clifford Chambers by a level fieldpath,
we go back to the Centre by road.

Families who prefer to break the walk at the Shire Horse Centre can start from
Atherstone.

Attractions
Stratford upon Avon Shire Horse Centre and Farm Park (open all year) occupies
the 360-acre Forge Farm by the little River Stour at Clifford Chambers. A real
family attraction, its emphasis is on "the gentle giants of agriculture" – the great
Shire horses that pulled wagons and ploughs in pre-mechanized days. A dozen of
them demonstrate their working skills and provide wagon rides. There are also
children's pony rides, a riverside nature trail and a large collection of rare breeds of
farm animals. The restaurant is open to non-visitors.

Clifford Chambers is a lovely village with no through traffic. Its name stems
from the Chamberer or Chamberlain of the Abbot of Gloucester, who administered
the manor in the Middle Ages. The splendid Manor House stands at the end of the
main street and there is a fine black and white gabled rectory beside the Norman
church, which was restored in 1886.

The walk to Preston on Stour provides striking views of the Cotswolds. Try to
spot the tower on Broadway Hill, eleven miles away. Preston is another attractive
village, with a church mainly rebuilt in the 1750s by James West of Alscot Park. We
get a good view of West's Gothic Revival mansion, before reaching straggling
Atherstone on Stour. There the Victorian Gothic church has long been disused and
pigeons coo in its tower.

Refreshments
Restaurant at Shire Horse Centre; inn at Clifford Chambers.

Route 15

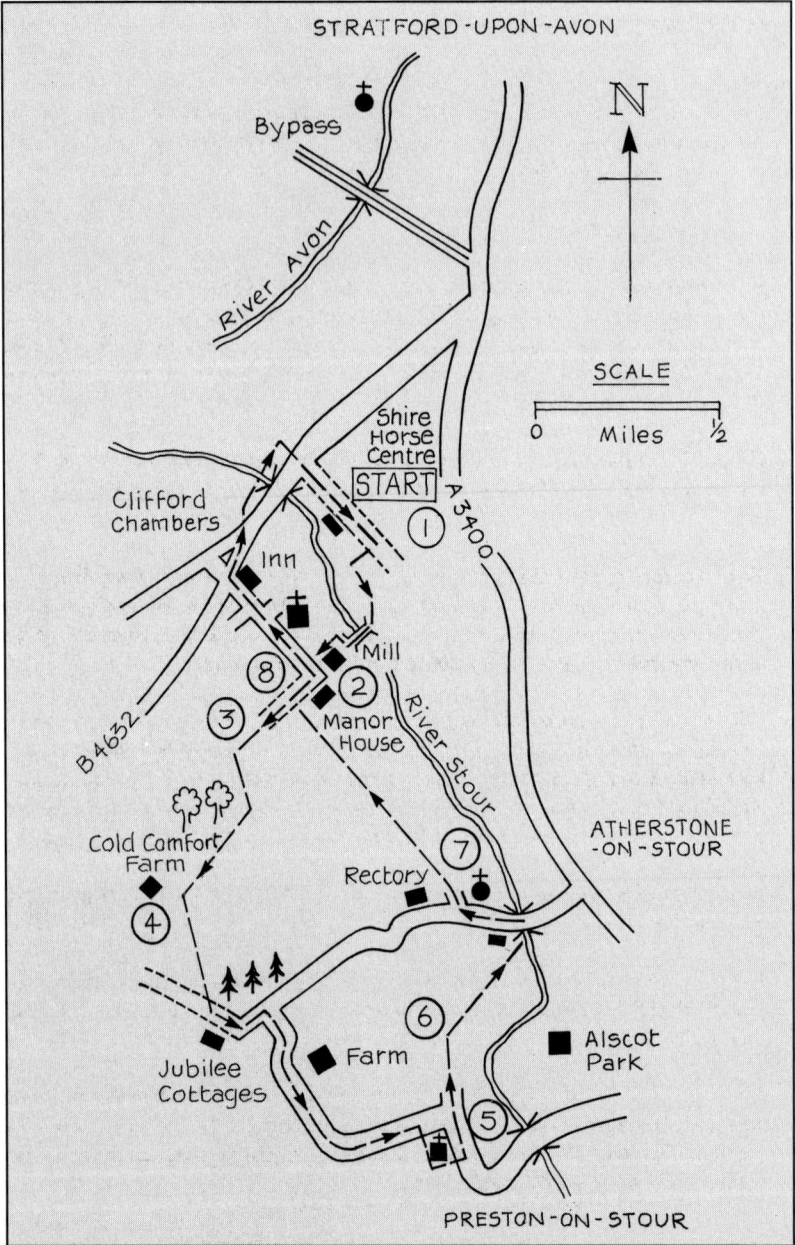

STRATFORD-UPON-AVON

Bypass

River Avon

N

SCALE
0   Miles   ½

Shire
Horse
Centre
START

①

A 3400

Clifford
Chambers

Inn

Mill

②

⑧

③

Manor
House

River Stour

B 4632

Cold Comfort
Farm

④

Rectory

⑦

ATHERSTONE
-ON-STOUR

⑥

Alscot
Park

Jubilee
Cottages

Farm

⑤

PRESTON-ON-STOUR

Route 15

Stratford Shire Horse Centre   6 miles

Start

Car-park, Shire Horse Centre, off B4632 (formerly A46), 2 miles south of Stratford upon Avon (OS Sheet 151 GR 199527). Walkers not visiting the Centre can park on the roadside at Clifford Chambers or Atherstone on Stour.

Route

1. From the Centre, follow the track away from the B4632 for about 100 yards to a waymarked gateway on the right. Take the public path through the Centre's land to a stile leading into a meadow, and turn left along a fence. Towards the end of the field veer right to a stile, cross to a kissing gate beyond a telegraph pole, and go over the River Stour footbridge.

2. A fenced path skirts a fish farm and – passing an old mill, its water-wheel visible on the far side – reaches the Manor House gates at the end of Clifford Chambers' main street.

3. Take the track opposite and pass through a gate. Where the track swings left, leave it to climb beside the right-hand hedge to a wood. Skirt to the left and go up to a gate. Continue right of a hedge to a gap, near the top of the rise, then left of the hedge downhill to a field corner above Cold Comfort Farm.

4. Turn left along the bottom of the field and, at the next corner, pass between hedge and fence to step over wire-netting on the right into a sloping field. Follow the high ground to a stile near the end of a forestry plantation and go left up an unmade lane. At Jubilee Cottages bear briefly left to a surfaced by-way, turn right to Preston on Stour, and follow a broad green walk on the right to the back gate of the church.

5. Leaving the church by the front gate, descend the village green, and turn left along a lane that soon narrows to become a path leading to a kissing gate into Alscot Park.

6. With the house visible below, the path crosses sheep pastures to a gate left of a large grassy mound. Skirt a fenced plantation to the next gate, turn right, and follow an enclosed path to a lane at Atherstone on Stour.

7. Go left, past the disused church, to a bend, and take a farm track ahead, with the flat-roofed Georgian rectory to the left. Keeping straight on, the way becomes a beaten fieldpath leading to a small brick building, then a fenced path ending at the track by which we left Clifford Chambers.

Continued on page 70

69

8. *Back in the village, walk down the main street to the New Inn at the far end and bear right to the B4632. Follow its footpath to the right, over the River Stour, and take a surfaced track on the right back to the Shire Horse Centre.*

Access by bus
From Stratford upon Avon to Clifford Chambers and Preston on Stour.

Ready for a wagon ride at the Shire Horse Centre

The Battle of Edgehill

Outline
Nadbury Camp – Ratley – Edge Hill – Radway – Arlescote – Nadbury Camp

Summary
Varied and quite hilly walking along fieldpaths, a bridleway and quiet lanes, in lovely countryside. There are ancient stone villages in the valleys, and we cross the hill that gave its name to the first battle of the English Civil War.

Attractions
If approaching Edge Hill along the B4086 from Kineton, you will pass a roadside memorial, a mile from the town. It tells us that many who died in the famous battle on the Sunday afternoon of October 23, 1642, were buried on the battlefield, ¾-mile to the south. Ironically, we are forbidden to walk where the fighting occurred, because the area has been taken over by the Ministry of Defence. There are, however, reminders of the battle on this walk. There is also a Battle of Edgehill Museum at Farnborough House (National Trust, 4 miles east).

When the battle took place, the landscape looked very different. The woods that clothe the ridge had not been planted and there was only one hedgerow between the hill and Kineton. Fought between troops commanded by King Charles I and his nephew, Prince Rupert, on the Royalist side, and by the Earl of Essex for the Parliamentarians, it lasted barely three hours on that sunlit autumn afternoon. Early honours went to the King's men, who descended the hillside and passed south of Radway to attack the Roundheads and force them back to Kineton, but Essex rallied and nightfall brought the fighting to an inconclusive end.

The Castle Inn (formerly Radway Tower) on Edge Hill, was built about 1750 by Sanderson Miller to mark the spot where King Charles raised his standard before the battle. A pioneer of the Gothic revival in architecture, Miller lived below at Radway Grange, a Tudor house, which he greatly altered. Radway Church, which in 1866 replaced an earlier building whose ancient graveyard we pass on entering the village, contains the monument of Captain Henry Kingsmill of Kent, one of 1,200 soldiers killed in the battle.

At Arlescote – below Knowle End, from which King Charles surveyed Essex's position with a telescope – is a charming little stone-built manor house of Tudor origin. Here the King's young sons, the future Charles II and James II, stayed during the battle. The quaint, ogee-roofed gazebos, or turrets, were added during 17th century alterations, in which the great architect Inigo Jones played a part.

Interesting man-made landscape features seen on the walk include the 18-acre Bronze Age hillfort beside the B4086 at the start and old ridge and furrow field systems on each side of the lane to Arlescote.

Route 16

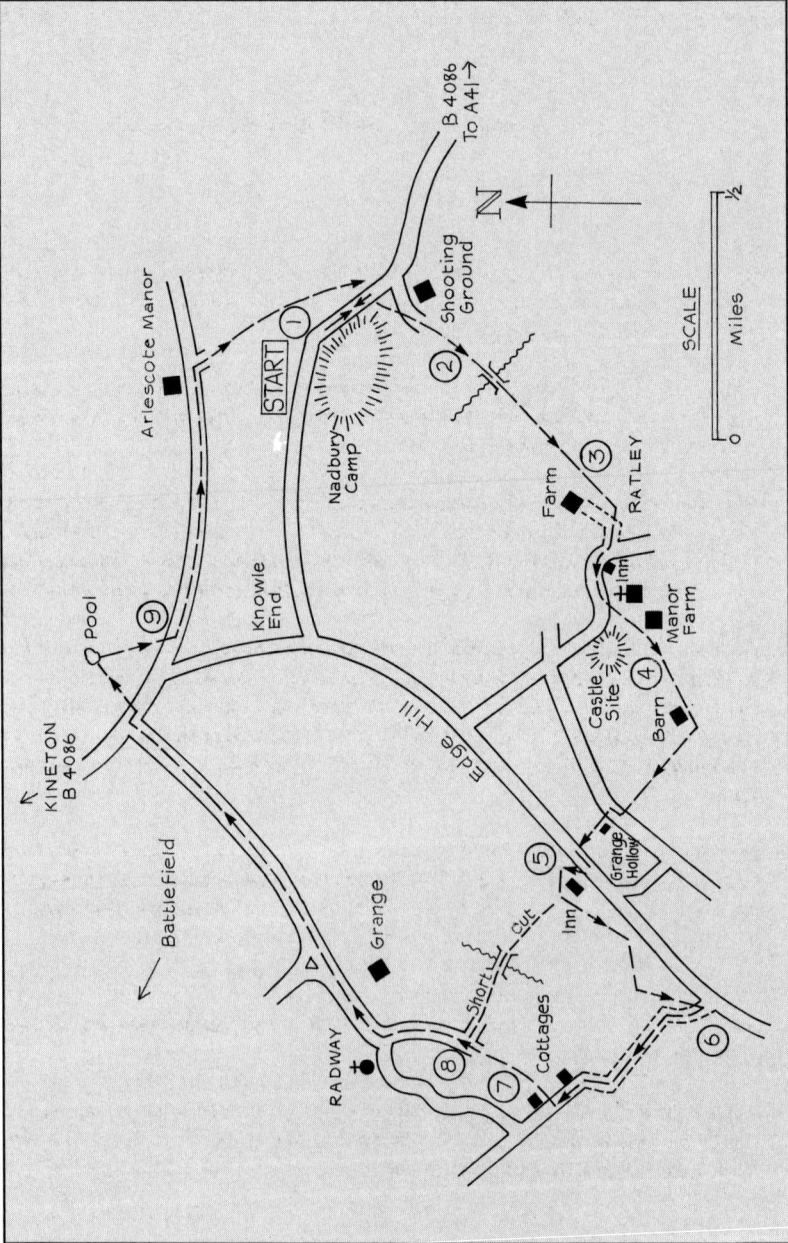

Route 16

The Battle of Edgehill

5½ miles

Start

From lay-by at sharp bend on B4086, by Nadbury Camp (OS Sheet 151 GR 391484).

Route

1. *Heading south-east, enter a fieldgate on the right (just before Edge Hill Shooting Ground), cross to an exit gate on the far side, and descend a concreted track to a gate leading into a sloping field.*

2. *Go down beside the hedge on the right and over corner fencing. Descend to a broad gap in the bottom hedge, and climb to a stile at the top right corner of a field, then to a gate at the top of the next one.*

3. *Skirt a farmhouse fence to a stile at a bend on its drive, which drops steeply into Ratley. The mottes, or mounds, of the castle site are well seen across the village as you descend. Pass the Rose & Crown to a small green and bear left. Climb past the church to a larger green, and turn left to a stone stile near the gate of Manor Farm.*

4. *Go over a rise by the fenced-off castle site, and descend its far side. Turn right to a stile/gate, and climb to a stile by a corrugated-iron barn at the top of the field. Bear right along a track to a lane, passing a nature reserve on a former quarry site. Turn right and, beyond the gateway of Grange Hollow, take an enclosed path on the left that emerges right of the Castle Inn on the road that runs along the crest of Edge Hill.*

5. *Just short of the inn, a path on the right descends to a stile. (From it, a quick descent to Radway, avoiding a possibly muddy bridleway, can be made by following the path left of hedges.) For the full walk, however, ignore the stile and continue parallel to the road along a wooded path.*

6. *After about ⅓ mile, the path meets a bridleway, King John's Lane, which can be very muddy. Descend it to a cottage and, immediately before a second cottage, turn right through a fieldgate.*

7. *Follow the left field-edge past a kissing gate to a corner stile. Next, go along the right-hand field-edge to a stile and an enclosed path, bordered by ancient tombstones, ending at a green in Radway.*

Continued on page 74

73

8. *Keep ahead along a lane to a junction near the church, bear right to reach the B4086 and turn right. Here road-walking can be avoided by climbing a stile on the far side, bearing half-right across a field with a pronounced ridge and furrow system to a fenced pool, and turning sharp right, uphill, to a stile at a road junction.*

9. *Go left up the lane to Arlescote. At the Manor House, turn right beyond a green and take a track between a fence and a converted barn to a gate. Follow a green track uphill to the right and later fork right, again uphill. Ignore a gate to the B4086, continue along a grassy terrace and cross a stile to the road, opposite the shooting ground. Turn right to the lay-by.*

Access by bus
No regular public transport, but David R. Grasby Coaches (tel 0926-640455) run Thursday and Saturday services between Kineton and Banbury, via Ratley.

Refreshments   Rose & Crown, Ratley; Castle Inn, Edge Hill.

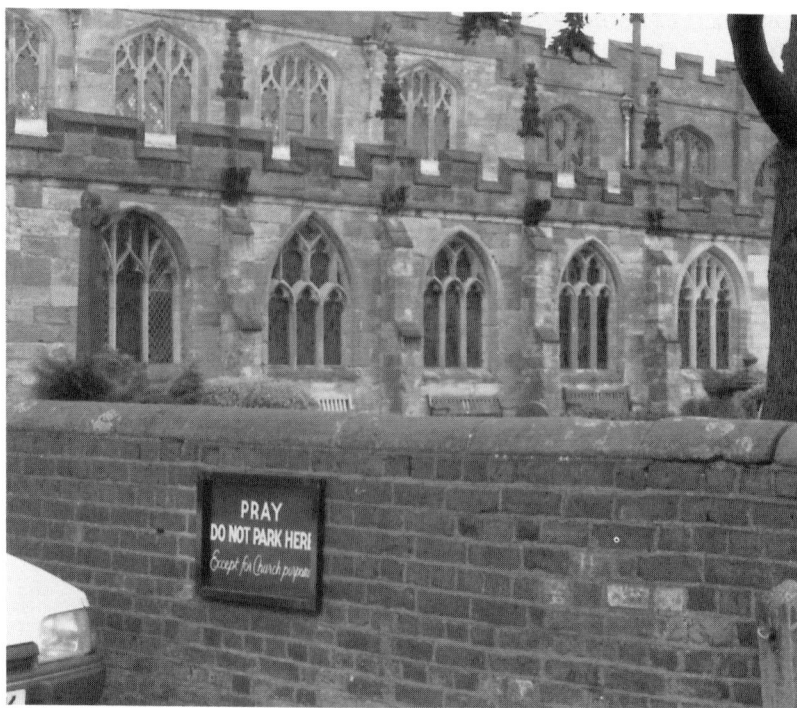

. . . and a final message from the ecclesiastical authorities at Knowle

74

Useful information

Routes in order of difficulty

None of these walks is through rough or very hilly country, but the following is an approximate indication of their respective standards.

Easy walks – fairly level going throughout:
Route 3 – *Kingsbury Water Park*   (*4 miles*)
Route 5 – *Birmingham Canals*   (*4¼ miles*)
Route 6 – *Sarehole Mill and the River Cole*   (*3 miles*)
Route 11 – *Coombe Abbey and its Bridleways*   (*1½ or 5¼ miles*)

Walks with some gentle climbing:
Route 9 – *Kenilworth Castle and The Pleasance*   (*4 or 6 miles*)
Route 12 – *Clowes Wood and Earlswood Lakes*   (*4 or 6½ miles*)

Hillier walks, but no steep gradients:
Route 1 – *Alvecote Priory and Pools*   (*4 or 5 miles*)
Route 2 – *Sutton Park*   (*6½ miles*)
Route 7 – *Knowle and Temple Balsall*   (*5½ miles*)
Route 8 – *Berkswell and its Windmill*   (*5½ miles*)
Route 10 – *Stoneleigh and Baginton: Romans and Countrymen*   (*5 miles*)
Route 14 – *Warwick: Castle, Canal and Countryside*   (*6 miles*)

Longer walks with steeper climbs or several hills:
Route 4 – *Hartshill Hayes and the Centenary Way*   (*3¼ or 9 miles*)
Route 13 – *Henley's Castle Mount*   (*7 miles*)
Route 15 – *Stratford Shire Horse Centre*   (*6 miles*)
Route 16 – *The Battle of Edgehill*   (*5½ miles*)

Public transport – Warwickshire and the West Midlands

British Rail. Tel 021-643-2711

Bus Information:
Centro Hotline. Tel 021-200-2700
West Midlands Travel. Tel 021-236-8313
Midland Red North. Tel Tamworth 63861
Midland Red West. Tel 021-200-2700
  Worcester 359393

Tourist information centres in Warwickshire and the West Midlands

Birmingham. BCVP Ticket Shop and Information Office, City Arcade. Tel 021-643-2514.
  Central Library. Tel 021-235-4651.
National Exhibition Centre. Tel 021-780-4321.
Birmingham Airport. Information Desk. Tel 021-767-7145/6.
Birmingham International Convention Centre. Tel 021-665-6116.
Coventry. Bayley Lane. Tel 0203-832303.
Kenilworth. The Library, 11 Smalley Place. Tel 0926-52595/50708.
Leamington Spa. The Jephson Lodge, Jephson Gardens, The Parade. Tel 0926-311470.
Nuneaton. The Library, Church Street. Tel 0203-384027.
Rugby. The Library, St Matthew Street. Tel. 0788-535348.
Solihull. Central Library, Homer Road. Tel 021-704-6130.
Stratford-upon-Avon. Bridgefoot. Tel 0789-293127/294466.
Warwick. The Court House, Jury Street. Tel 0926-492212.

Wet weather alternatives – completely or partly under cover (admission free where stated). It is advisable to check times of opening. For attractions in Birmingham and Coventry refer to local tourist information offices.

Museums, Galleries and Craft Workshops

Abbey Barn, Abbey Fields, Kenilworth. Norman stonework from Abbey ruins, tiles, gargoyles, farm and tannery tools, local finds. Admission free. Tel 0926-53574.

Antique Doll Collection. Golden Cross Inn, Wixford Road, Ardens Grafton, near Bidford-on-Avon. Admission free. Tel 0789-772420.

Berkswell Museum. Berkswell village. Local memorabilia, implements, etc. Tel 0676-33322/32371/33678.

Edgehill Battle Museum. The Estate Yard, Farnborough Hall, near Banbury. Armour, costumes, etc, of Battle of Edgehill, 1642. Tel 0295-89593 or 0296-332213.

James Gilbert Rugby Football Museum. St Matthew's Street, Rugby. Rugby memorabilia. Shop where balls made since 1842. Admission free. Tel 0788-536500.

Leamington Spa Art Gallery and Museum. Avenue Road. Paintings, pottery and local history. Admission free. Tel 0926-426559.

Manor Farm Craft Centre. Wood Lane, Earlswood. Craft workshop, farm shop, homemade ice-cream, tea room. Admission free. Tel 05646-2729.

Middleton Hall Craft Centre, near Tamworth. Working craftsmen and women. Admission free.

Midland Air Museum. Coventry Airport, Baginton. Over 20 historic aircraft. Sir Frank Whittle Jet Heritage Centre. Tel 0203-301033.

Museum of Country Bygones. Louisa Ward Close, off High Street, Marton, near Leamington Spa. Craftsmen's tools, household and dairy equipment and wagons.

National Motorcycle Museum. On A45 at Bickenhill. 600 British machines from 1898 onwards. Tel 06755-3311.

Nuneaton Library. Church Street. Local history collection and George Eliot photographs, letters books, etc. Admission free. Tel 0203-384027/347006.

Nuneaton Museum and Art Gallery. Riversley Park. Local history, archaeology, art and the George Eliot Collection. Admission free. Tel 0203-350595.

Oldwych Gallery, Oldwych House Farm, Fen End, Kenilworth. Paintings by Midlands artists. Admission free. Tel 0676-33552.

Rugby Library and Exhibition Gallery. St Matthew's Street. Loan exhibitions and local artists. Admission free.

St John's House. Coten End, Warwick. Branch of county museum and Royal Warwickshire Regiment Museum. Admission free. Tel 0926-410410, ext 2021.

Teddy Bear Museum. 19 Greenhill Street, Stratford-upon-Avon. Hundreds of teddies in Elizabethan setting.

Warwickshire Museum. Market Place, Warwick. County museum. History, geology, Sheldon's great tapestry map, etc. Admission free. Tel 0926-410410, ext 2500.

Warwickshire Yeomanry Museum. The Court House, Jury Street, Warwick. Uniforms, arms, swords, etc. See also The Court House below. Admission free. Tel 0926-492212.

Wellesbourne Watermill. Mill Farm, Wellesbourne, near Stratford-upon-Avon. Waterwheel, machinery, video, teas.

Wellesbourne Wartime Museum. Former Wellesbourne Mountford RAF station. World War II relics, in underground bunker. Battle operations control room. Admission free.

Castles, Houses and Churches

Anne Hathaway's Cottage. Shottery, near Stratford-upon-Avon. Thatched farmhouse, home of Shakespeare's wife. Tel 0789-292100.

Arbury Hall, near Nuneaton. Unique example of Gothic Revival. Tel 0203-382804.

Baddesley Clinton, near Lapworth. National Trust. Moated medieval manor house. Tel 0564-783294.

Charlecote Park, near Stratford-upon-Avon. National Trust. Elizabethan, Tudor gatehouse, deer park. Tel 0789-470277.

Chester House. Knowle Library, 1667–9 High Street, Knowle. Elizabethan town house, with parts from 1400. Admission free. Tel 0564-775840.

Collegiate Church of St Mary. Old Square, Warwick. 15th century Beauchamp Chapel, Norman crypt. Admission free. Tel 0926-400771.

Coughton Court, near Alcester. National Trust. Mainly Elizabethan. Gunpowder Plot connection. Tel 0789-762435.

The Court House. Jury Street, Warwick. 18th century Italian style, including Mayor's Parlour and Ballroom. Also Warwickshire Yeomanry Museum (see above). Admission free. Tel 0926-492212.

Farnborough Hall, near Banbury. National Trust. Classical 18th century.

Ragley Hall, near Alcester. 17th century Palladian. Tel 0789-762090.

Hall's Croft. Old Town, Stratford-upon-Avon. Tudor town house, home of Shakespeare's daughter and doctor son-in-law. Tel 0789-292107.

Harvard House. High Street, Stratford-upon-Avon. Rebuilt 1596. Early home of Katherine Rogers, mother of John Harvard (founder of Harvard University, USA). Tel 0789-204507.

Holy Trinity Church. Old Town, Stratford-upon-Avon. Lovely riverside setting. Graves of William Shakespeare and Anne Hathaway. Admission free, but charge to view Shakespeare's grave. Tel 0789-266316.

Lord Leycester Hospital. High Street, Warwick. Old soldiers' home since 1571. Chapel, Great Hall and Guildhall. Tel 0926-491422.

New Place/Nash's House. Chapel Street, Stratford-upon-Avon. Foundations of Shakespeare's last home in Elizabethan garden. Period furniture and museum of Stratford's history. Tel 0789-292325.

Packwood House, near Lapworth. National Trust. Timber-framed Tudor. Famous yew garden. Tel 0564-782024.

Shakespeare's Birthplace. Henley Street, Stratford-upon-Avon. Half-timbered, with many original features. Shakespearean books, manuscripts, etc. Tel 0789-204016.

Shakespeare Countryside Museum and Mary Arden's House. Wilmcote, near Stratford-upon-Avon. Tudor farmstead. Museum of rural life and home of Shakespeare's mother. Tel 0789-293455.

Tamworth Castle and Museum. Norman Keep, Tudor Chapel, Jacobean State Apartments. Locally minted Saxon coin collection. Tel 0827-63563.

Upton House, Edgehill. National Trust. Late 17th century. Outstanding collection of paintings. Tel 029587-266.

Warwick Castle. England's finest medieval castle. Many rooms, including Great Hall and Dungeon. Madame Tussaud tableau of "A Royal Weekend Party – 1898". Tel 0926-495421.

Warwick Doll Museum. Oken's House. Collection of antique dolls, dolls' houses, toys, etc. Tel 0926-495546 or 410410, ext 2500.

Other Places of Interest

Ashorne Hall Nickelodeon. Ashorne Hill, near Warwick. Collection of mechanical musical instruments. Live show on Sundays. Tel 0926-651444.

Berkswell Windmill. Windmill Lane, Balsall Common. Tower mill, with original machinery (not working). Tel 0676-33403.

Jardinerie. Kenilworth Road, Hampton-in-Arden. Garden centre, aquatic centre and coffee shop. Admission free. Tel 06755-2866.

Napton Windmill. Napton-on-the-Hill, near Southam.

Notcutts Garden Centre. Large covered sales area, childrens' playground, licenced restaurant. Admission free. Tel 021-744-4501.

Splashland. Tudor Grange Swimming Centre, Blossomfield Road, Solihull. High-speed waterslide, bobsled run, childrens' area. Tel 021-704-5206.

Stratford Brass Rubbing Centre. Summerhouse, Royal Shakespeare Theatre, Avonbank Gardens. Unique collection of brass rubbing. Admission free. Tel 0789-297671.

Stratford-upon-Avon Butterfly Farm. Tramway Walk. Europe's largest live butterfly safari. Tel 0789-299288.

Twycross Zoo. Twycross, east of Tamworth. Finest primate collection in the country (the Typhoo chimps), etc. Tel 0827-880250.

Tysoe Windmill. Tysoe, south-west of Edgehill.

Bibliography

Just a selection of useful publications, past and present.

Guide to English Heritage Properties – English Heritage.
The National Trust Handbook – The National Trust.
Places to Visit in the Heart of England – The Heart of England Tourist Board.
History, People and Places in Warwickshire – Harold Parsons, 1975.
Warwickshire – Vivian Bird, 1973.
A Short History of Warwickshire and Birmingham – Vivian Bird, 1977.
Warwickshire: Shakespeare's County – Arthur Mee, 1936 (republished 1991).
The Buildings of England; Warwickshire – Nikolaus Pevsner.
In the Forest of Arden – John Burman, 1948.
Rambles Round the Edge Hills and in the Vale of the Red Horse – George Miller, 1896 (republished 1967).
The Centenary Way – Warwickshire County Council (11 leaflets).
Sutton Park; Its History and Wildlife – Douglas V. Jones.
Warwick Castle – Official Guide.
Walking around Stoneleigh in Arden – Audrey V. Gilbert, 1991.
Birmingham and Fazeley Canal – Birmingham Canal Walkway Guides. No. 1: Gas Street Basin to Aston Junction.
Digbeth Canal – As above, No. 3: Aston Junction to Warwick Bar.
Nicholson's Guides to the Waterways, 5: Midlands – Robert Nicholson Publications.

Radway Tower (Route 16)

THE FAMILY WALKS SERIES

Family Walks on Anglesey. Laurence Main. ISBN 0 907758 665.
Family Walks in Berkshire & North Hampshire. Kathy Sharp. ISBN 0 907758 371.
Family Walks around Bristol, Bath & the Mendips. Nigel Vile. ISBN 0 907758 193.
Family Walks around Cardiff & the Valleys. Gordon Hindess. ISBN 0 907758 541.
Family Walks in Cheshire. Chris Buckland. ISBN 0 907758 290.
Family Walks in Cornwall. John Caswell. ISBN 0 907758 55X.
Family Walks in the Cotswolds. Gordon Ottewell. ISBN 0 907758 150.
Family Walks on Exmoor & the Quantocks. John Caswell. ISBN 0 907758 460.
Family Walks in South Gloucestershire. Gordon Ottewell. ISBN 0 907758 339.
Family Walks in Gower. Amanda Green. ISBN 0 907758 630.
Family Walks in Hereford and Worcester. Gordon Ottewell. ISBN 0 907758 207.
Family Walks on the Isle of Wight. Laurence Main. ISBN 0 907758 568.
Family Walks in North West Kent. Clive Cutter. ISBN 0 907758 363.
Family Walks in the Lake District. Barry McKay. ISBN 0 907758 401.
Family Walks in Mendip, Avalon & Sedgemoor. Nigel Vile. ISBN 0 907758 41X.
Family Walks in the New Forest. Nigel Vile. ISBN 0 907758 606.
Family Walks in Oxfordshire. Laurence Main. ISBN 0 907758 38X.
Family Walks in the Dark Peak. Norman Taylor. ISBN 0 907758 169.
Family Walks in the White Peak. Norman Taylor. ISBN 0 907758 096.
Family Walks in South Derbyshire. Gordon Ottewell. ISBN 0 907758 614.
Family Walks in South Shropshire. Marian Newton. ISBN 0 907758 304.
Family Walks in Snowdonia. Laurence Main. ISBN 0 907758 320.
Family Walks in the Staffordshire Peaks and Potteries. Les Lumsdon. ISBN 0 907758 347.
Family Walks around Stratford & Banbury. Gordon Ottewell. ISBN 0 907758 495.
Family Walks in Suffolk. C J Francis. ISBN 0 907758 649.
Family Walks around Swansea. Raymond Humphreys. ISBN 0 907758 622.
Family Walks in the Teme Valley. Camilla Harrison. ISBN 0 907758 452.
Family Walks in Three Peaks & Malham. Howard Beck. 428.
Family Walks in Mid Wales. Laurence Main. ISBN 0 907758 274.
Family Walks in the North Wales Borderlands. Gordon Emory. ISBN 0 907758 509.
Family Walks in Warwickshire. Geoff Allen. ISBN 0 907758 533.
Family Walks in the Weald of Kent & Sussex. Clive Cutter. ISBN 0 907758 517.
Family Walks in Wiltshire. Nigel Vile. ISBN 0 907758 215.
Family Walks in the Wye Valley. Heather & Jon Hurley. ISBN 0 907758 266.
Family Walks in the North Yorkshire Dales. Howard Beck. ISBN 0 907758 525.
Family Walks in South Yorkshire. Norman Taylor. ISBN 0 907758 258.
Family Walks in West Yorkshire. Howard Beck. ISBN 0 907758 436.

The publishers welcome suggestions for further titles in this series; and will be pleased to consider manuscripts relating to Derbyshire from new or established authors.

Scarthin Books of Cromford, in the Peak District, are also leading second-hand and antiquarian booksellers, and are eager to purchase specialised material, both ancient and modern.
Contact Dr D. J. Mitchell, 0629-823272.